Sea Liverpool

The Maritime Art of Edward D Walker

Text: Dr Adrian Jarvis

This book is dedicted to the memory of my parents

Ted and Bella Walker

also the late George H Tulloch (a great American)

First edition published in in Great Britain 2006 by Ron Jones Associates.

ISBN 0–9511703–6–8

Designed and published by Ron Jones Associates Limited.
(Email: publishing@rja-mpl.com)

Printed and bound in Spain.

CONTENTS

ACKNOWLEDGEMENTS

This book would not have been possible without financial sponsorship from the Ethel Austin Property Group.

Edward D Walker would like to thank the following friends and colleagues who have given valuable assistance, advice and encouragement over the years.

Mr & Mrs George H Tulloch, USA
Charles & Bea Haas, USA
John P. Eaton, USA
Matt Tulloch
Captain P.H. Nargeolet Retrd., French Navy
Joe Carvalho, USA
Fred Robinson Jr.
Mr & Mrs Nigel Green
Mr & Mrs Douglas Elliot
Eric Flounders, Cunard Shipping Co.
Michael Gallagher, Cunard Shipping Co.
Gerry Ellis, Cunard Shipping Co.
Captain Robin Woodall Retrd. R.D*R.N.R., Cunard
Barry Owen and Andrew Lovelady, Ethel Austin Property Group
Peter Elson, Liverpool Daily Post
Dr Adrian Jarvis
Alan Brack
Oriel Studios, Merseyside
Mr & Mrs Peter Waters
Gilbert Upton
Les Rawlinson
Brian McShane, M.D.H.C
Steve Gallimore, M.D.H.C
Mr & Mrs Michael Whelan, Cobh, Co Cork
Mr & Mrs Frank Barnes
Mr & Mrs Geoff Walker
Gerry Williams
Richard Nicholson, Christleton
Alex Murdoch

EDWARD D WALKER

He is the man who stands at his easel all day in an unassuming semi-detached house on the outskirts of Merseyside. But come the star-climbed night, embarked aboard his dreams, he sails away in his mind on ships through the oceans of time and space.

Perhaps that is why even the most dedicated landlubber viewing Edward D Walker's maritime paintings in this book can practically smell the brine on the breeze and feel the salt spray cake on their cheeks. Vessels, supposedly frozen in his oils, convey an uncanny dynamic, wallowing, pitching and rolling as they butt through the foaming waves. Sails billow and undulate, as if taunting the on-looker to reach out and punch the canvas. Viewers unconsciously square their footing, steadying their balance. Imagine, then, the impact on those who have enjoyed, or perhaps endured, a life on the ocean wave.

None are immune. King Juan Carlos of Spain was guest of honour at the Columbus 500 celebration during the 1992 Tall Ships Race in Liverpool and was presented with a Ted Walker painting of the city's world famous waterfront. Dominating the foreground the artist depicted the premier Spanish sail training ship, *Juan Sebastian de Elcano*, aboard which the king had served as a cadet while heir apparent. Later, Ted asked a royal aide how the painting was received by the king, by now back aboard his old ship. He replied: "When I left His Majesty, he had it propped up in his cabin. He was just gazing at it with his head resting on his hands."

When Deputy Prime Minister and former Cunard Line steward John Prescott was asked what he would like as thanks for co-sponsoring the renaming of the company's *Caronia* at Liverpool's Princes Landing Stage, he replied: "A Ted Walker painting of my favourite ship, *Franconia*, please."

What makes this unassuming grandfather so special is his gift for producing paintings that would silence the most pernickety rivet-counter and yet are works of art which soar above mere photo-realism. His research is meticulous, ably-assisted by his wife Susan, who delves into the background which underpins each painting, unearthing plans, documents, contemporary logs, pictures, contacts and organising fact-finding trips.

The outcome of such painstaking investigation are paintings such as the rescue of the ailing barque *Mexico*, off Southport. Aboard the Lytham lifeboat, while being rowed up perpendicular walls of boiling water, the coxswain messianically holds high a baton, to which a life-line is attached for the gaping souls upon the *Mexico*. These details came from eye-witness accounts.

Ted has also established a network of experts to consult, such as his friend Captain Robin Woodall, of Hoylake. A former Cunard Line Commodore, Captain Woodall commanded *QE2* on her inaugural visit to Liverpool in 1990, commemorating the company's founding here 150 years earlier.

Ted is a deeply spiritual man who both prays for guidance and follows his heart. He feels imbued with the experiences and emotions of his forebears who, as captains and crew, courageously plied the seven seas in the days of sail.

He has traced his family back to 1617. His maternal grandfather came from Stornoway, in Outer Hebrides, but was shipwrecked on a sailing ship in the North Sea. After marrying the daughter of the sea captain who rescued him, they settled in her Hartlepool hometown. This grandfather was later a Royal Naval stoker on the iron-clad warships. Ted's paternal great-grandfather was a captain under sail, with generations of his family serving at sea.

This innate memory of collected emotions from his antecedents seems to course through his arms and onto the canvases, appropriately via the medium of a pallet knife given to him 40 years ago by his mother. Perhaps this is why seas and skies pour forth from him: seas that are boiling, wrinkled, glassy, serpent-haunted, rough-rude and unplumbed. Each wave an individual contributing by their hundreds to a magnificent whole. Skies that frame breaking grey dawns or golden, shining days. Cloud-suspended, or wild and windswept skies; clear and bitter nights and freezing, haunted fogs.

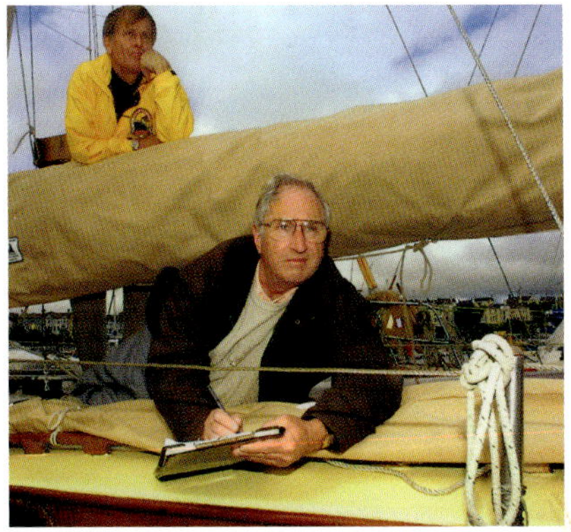

Ted with his close friend George Tulloch just before setting sail on a research trip from Bangor, N. Ireland, into the Irish Sea. "George was a dreamer – I painted his dreams".

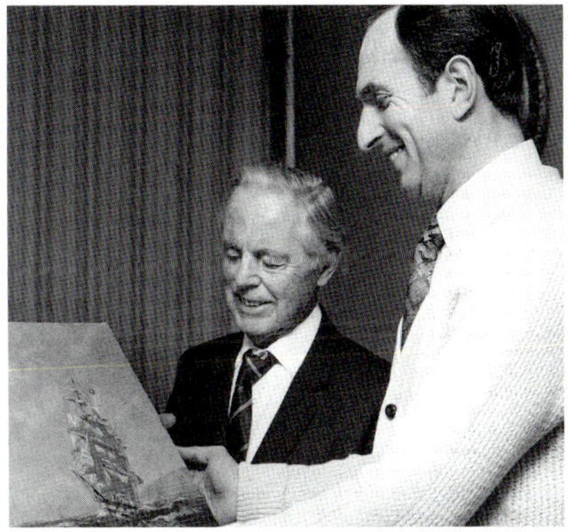

The artist with Cdr. Stuart Cross RCNC, FRINA, C.Eng. O.B.E. They became great friends over the years, Stuart becoming honorary grandpa to the Walker children, Martin and Suzanne. Stuart designed `HMS Plymouth` of Falklands fame. He was also a leading designer of the Leander Class frigate. Stuart is seen admiring a painting of his father's ship, `Nairnshire`.

By necessity he has mastered the seascape, as often the main subject of the ship comprises only a small portion of the canvas. "The sea is our master; elusive, threatening or silkily smooth - it has a multitude of colours, emotions and moods," says Ted. "Strangely, the success of a painting can often be decided by a smudge or flick of paint, the sunlight catching a cloud, reflections of light on a part of a ship or light reflecting on water. I'm always trying to do something new. I've even tried painting with a toothbrush to create a different effect."

After deciding on the subject matter, Ted next considers the composition: how the vessel would best be depicted, the angle, the weather conditions and location. Following this decision, the vessel is fitted in with the elements. The next stage involves drawing numerous sketches. Painting begins with the sky, built up layer by layer, similarly the sea and finally the ship itself.

His father initially worked in a Hartlepool shipyard, but because of the pre-war Depression, became a policeman and went into the prison service, eventually moving from Hull (where Ted was born in 1937) to Walton. "I could draw before I could walk. My parents used to shove a crayon or pencil into my hand to keep me busy," he recalls. "Even at that time I noticed things and had a built-in perspective. I always seemed to be drawing ships."

While he inherited his parents' love of the sea, his father's premature death forced him to leave Liverpool School of Art at 15 and into painting of a different kind for a living - decorating houses. A fall from a roof forced a change of direction into hair-dressing, followed by National Service and later running hardware shops. However, denying his powerful creative drive was increasingly stressful and some 40 years ago he plunged into maritime painting.

Ted and Susan's son and daughter, Martin and Suzanne, have grown up with the realisation that their father is a marine artist. His prestigious clients include Cunard Line and his paintings hang in the company's various offices worldwide. He illustrated Cunard's new flagship, *Queen Mary 2*, especially for a Royal Mail stamp. Often he is commissioned to cover official maritime events such as the 50th anniversary of the Battle of the Atlantic. Well-known in the USA, he has illustrated books by the maritime historians and *Titanic* experts John P Eaton and Charles Haas. Ted is noted for portraying both sides of the US Civil War, a conflict that deeply involved Liverpool through its trading links. His painting, *Shenandoah Surrendering in the River Mersey*, commemorates the last shot being fired in the Civil War.

Although a non-swimmer who is prone to *mal de mere*, Ted is simultaneously scared of water and bewitched by the element. Such is his dedication that he always takes to the water, whether in mill-pond conditions or a force 10 storm, whenever research demands it. No better example is his series of 15 paintings as official artist for the RMS *Titanic* Artefacts Touring Exhibition, showing the Liverpool-owned superliner at key points during her short, but notorious career. He insisted on photographing the Ulster coastline in rough waters off Bangor, passed decades earlier by the White Star flagship as what was the world's biggest ship departed from her Belfast birthplace at Harland & Wolff, in April, 1912.

In one of the many coincidences which litter his professional life, Ted sailed aboard *Vilia*, a yacht owned by the Talisker whiskey-distilling family. Built two years before the doomed *Titanic*, it is almost certain that *Vilia* witnessed her maiden sailing. Ted says: "I'm a great believer in fate and finding the spirit of the subject. I felt this on board the preserved tall ship *Moshulu*. She is now a permanently moored restaurant in Philadelphia, USA. Although she's strung up with fairy lights and has big windows cut into her hull sides, I felt I must paint this great wind-jammer and jumped around with excitement. When I got home, I just happened to pick a book off the shelf and it was *The Great Grain Race*, by the travel writer Eric Newby. There was a photo of *Moshulu*, on which he worked his passage to Australia and back. The resulting painting is probably my own favourite work."

"My first love has always been depicting deep-sea sailing vessels. A sailing ship is alive with creaking timbers and gusting sails, with a sweeping movement through a swelling sea. She is full of majesty, power and romance."

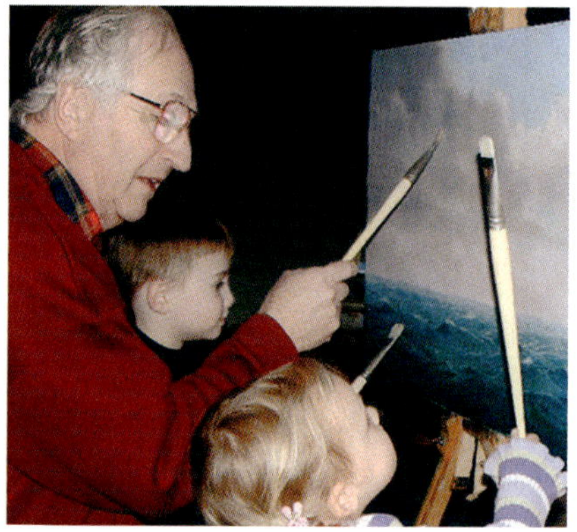

Artist with his grandchildren Freddy and Lucy, 2006.

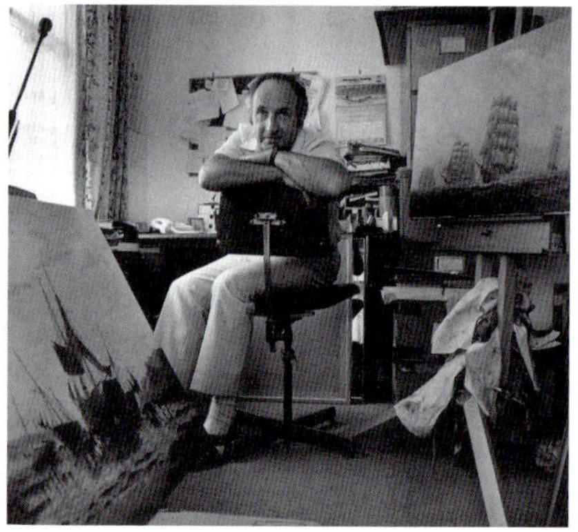

Artist in his studio.

On another occasion, Ted suffered painter's block while illustrating the Victorian square-rigger *Nairnshire*. Retreating for a short South coast holiday with his wife Susan, an unannounced couple called at their chalet enquiring after a lost cat. Espying Ted's maritime paintings in the hallway, they soon heard his woes about *Nairnshire*. The gentleman caller interrupted: "Ask me anything you like. My father was the captain of the *Nairnshire*."

Back home, refreshed and recharged, Ted suddenly had a premonition about the whereabouts of their new friends' cat, which led to its safe recovery. Most peculiarly, he left one of his *Titanic* paintings firmly clamped in place on his easel - only returning later to find the bolts loosened and the picture slipped off the stand, dangling at a 45° angle reminiscent of her final icy plunge.

Like any dedicated enthusiast, his chosen pathway embraces more than simply the work itself. Always ready to aid marine charities and especially those beleaguered souls, the ship preservationists, he has, for example, worked with (unpaid) gusto helping societies trying to preserve three key Merseyside vessels at their former home: *Planet*, *Whimbrel* and *Manxman*.

Planet was the last of the famous Mersey Bar lightships and Trinity House's last manned lightship. As Capt Robin Woodall says: "For every Mersey mariner, *Planet* was the unforgettable symbolic start or end to any voyage."

The former HMS *Whimbrel*, latterly owned by the Egyptian Navy as *Tariq*, is the sole-surviving Battle of the Atlantic warship. She served in the legendary Capt Johnnie Walker's U-boat hunter-killer second escort group, based at Liverpool's Gladstone and Canning Docks (as described in Liverpool writer Nicholas Monsarrat's novel *The Cruel Sea*).

Manxman is Britain's last traditional cross-channel steamer and was commissioned by the Isle of Man Steam Packet. Built at Cammell Laird, Birkenhead, *Manxman* is a scaled-down ocean liner, recalling Liverpool's lost passenger fleet, besides having carried millions of holidaymakers around the Irish Sea.

Encompassing an era from emigrant ships to the last Cammell Laird-built warships, via world-renowned vessels like those of Cunard, Blue Funnel, Harrison and Elder Dempster, this book graphically illustrates the Mersey's story as gateway to Liverpool, second city of the British Empire.

Yet this book is not a valedictory tribute to an artist past his prime. Ted Walker feels he is at his peak, having reached the point where the drive to make his vision a reality is matched by decades of practical experience perfecting his technique.

He still suffers from that dose of *Sea Fever* so eloquently described by John Masefield, himself a cadet aboard the Mersey training ship HMS *Conway*, whose poem ends:

"I must go down to the seas again, to the vagrant gypsy life,
To the gull's way and the whale's way where the wind's like a whetted knife:
And all I ask is a merry yarn from a laughing fellow-rover,
And quiet sleep and a sweet dream when the long trick's over."

Peter Elson
Senior Features Writer
Liverpool Daily Post

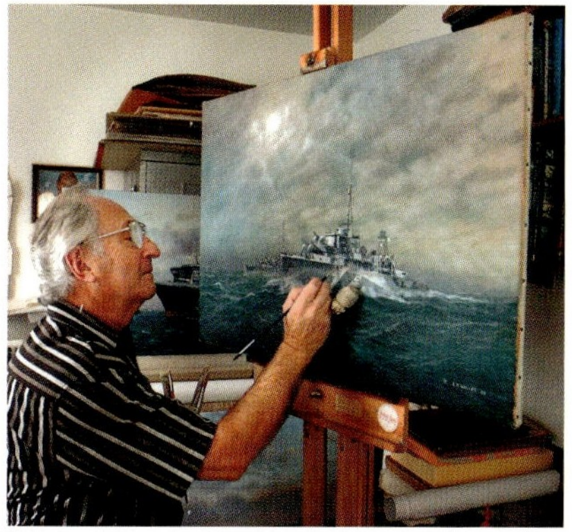

Ted puts the finishing touches to his 2006 painting of HMS Whimbrel.

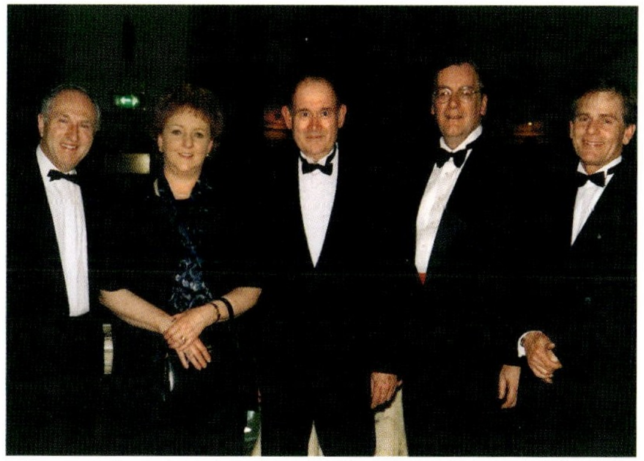

`RMS Titanic Team` at City Hall, Belfast. The artist with his wife Susan, John Eaton, Charles Haas and George Tulloch at a Titanic dinner in Belfast City Hall. (left to right)

A THUMBNAIL HISTORY OF THE PORT OF LIVERPOOL

I doubt whether the crown could possibly have been put on the head of a meaner coward, or a more detestable villain, if England had been searched from end to end to find him out. (Charles Dickens)

King John has not generally had a very good press, though some commentators have been more understanding than Charles Dickens, but in 1207 he bought the loyalty of Liverpudlians by creating the little settlement a borough and all its substantial citizens freemen, exempt from military service, roadmending and various other tiresome feudal duties. While he may not have been quite as bad as Dickens would have us believe, he was not likely to do this without looking for some return, and the return he wanted was an alternative to Chester should he wish to embark forces for Ireland without needing the aid of the Earl of Chester, who probably would have agreed with Dickens. It proved a good deal for the King, who successfully subdued Ireland in 1210, and it was a good deal for the citizens, who were newly enabled to manage their own communal affairs.

In so far as we can speak of a 'Port of Liverpool' in those early years, it was a 'port' artificially created for military, not economic, reasons and given the fairly hostile water conditions of the river it is hardly surprising that it was not immediately thronged with trading vessels. On the contrary, we have to wait until the sixteenth century before we find much growth in even Irish or coastwise trade and until 1648 for the first definite record of a transatlantic venture.

The late seventeenth century sees a noticeable gathering of pace, with Liverpool vessels growing both in number and in the ambition of their 'ventures'. This was partly due to earlier investment in such things as a public warehouse (1551) and the recent construction of the New Quay (1672), but the key development was the expansion of the coal and salt trades on the estuary, using coal from the St Helens coalfield to evaporate brine or purify rock salt, carry them on the Mersey to Liverpool and then export the finished product to Ireland, Newfoundland and many other places. The profits of the trade encouraged early investments in inland waterways, notably the Douglas and Weaver navigations, the Mersey and Irwell and the Sankey Canal which would stand Liverpool in good stead for other purposes too.

The Liverpool Corporation had quarrelled for generations with the Molyneux family (later the Earls of Sefton) but in 1872 a compromise was patched up to resolve their latest spat: Liverpool leased the Molyneux' manorial rights in the town, which provided a number of sources of revenue, notably the Town Dues which were payable on goods crossing the foreshore. Such a right could be used as loan security, and it was - to finance the construction of the world's first commercial wet dock, opened in 1715.

The first dock was not a huge and immediate success: history rarely works like that. It was a quiet and growing success, and behind the bald fact that an extra dock was not needed until 1753 lie many minor extension works to increase the capacity and the convenience of the port. By 1753, Liverpool traders were prominent around Europe, the West Indies and North America and were well embarked on their most notorious success, the achievement of hegemony in the trade in African Slaves. Nor was Liverpool any longer just a port: it was a burgeoning manufacturing centre as well, with glass houses, sugar houses, copper refineries and potteries. That new dock of 1753 was named Salthouse, for fairly obvious reasons. It should give us pause for thought, however, as to what was driving the growth of the port. Salt production needed four ingredients, two physical, two not. Liverpool had neither of the two physical ingredients, coal and salt, but it was strong in the two others, moving things around and connecting buyers with sellers through an effective merchant network. Those were what mattered.

For about half of the eighteenth century, Britain was at war with France. Each of those wars provided Liverpool with a trading bonus by encouraging the diversion of trade to the west coast ports, less accessible to French warships or privateers. Furthermore, Liverpool men's experience in the slave trade, using fairly small, fast-sailing ships helped them become effective privateers themselves. A successful cruise would yield life-changing sums of money to everyone from owner down to deckhand, which in the climate of the day was almost bound to be re-invested within the town. William Hutchinson, an ageing former Liverpool privateer, showed immaculate timing in publishing a book on how to be a successful privateer on the eve of the outbreak of the American War of Independence. Until Nelson laid the foundations of Pax Brittanica, not one of Liverpool's new docks was both proposed and completed when Britain was not at war.

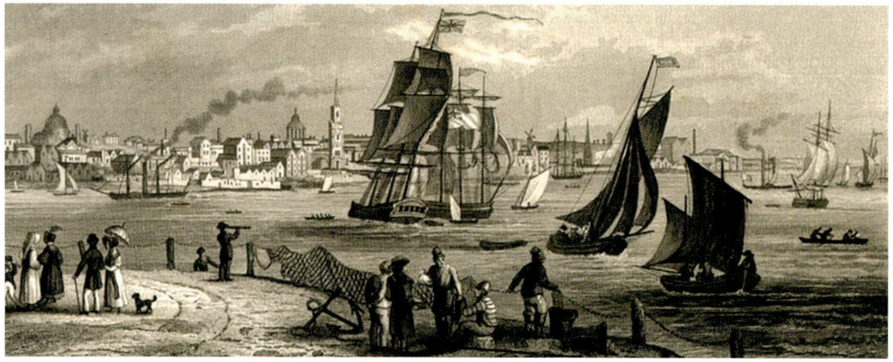

The year 1808 provided a major surprise: it had been widely expected that the abolition of the slave trade the previous year would ruin the port which had come to dominate it. Instead, Liverpool's trade reached a new record level. This was at least partly because few merchant houses or shipowners traded only in slaves and they had plenty of warning that they needed to concentrate on the other aspects of their business. By the time peace came in 1815, Liverpool men were to be found trading almost everywhere in the world, and within another decade they had consolidated ties with the newly-independent Latin American colonies of Spain and Portugal which would prove highly profitable and would last until the Falklands War. But many other trades were doing well: cotton was still growing fast, as was Canadian and other timber, while to the East, the end of the East India Company monopoly offered new opportunities to Liverpool men.

Scheduled passenger sailing packets on the North Atlantic appeared before 1820, but the trade was dominated from the American end. The beginning of steam driven mail services in 1840 handed the initiative to Liverpool, and the British superiority in iron and later steel shipbuilding consolidated it. The lead was only lost to Southampton after the turn of the century, by which time Liverpool liners were on virtually every route in the world, including a round-the-world route to Australia which could be used for any 'leg' of the voyage. But the glamour of the great liners should not conceal the fact that the lifeblood of the port was in the high-quality cargoliner business, where firms like Blue Funnel, T&J Harrison and Elder Dempster were pre-eminent until the Great War.

During the war much of this trade was lost to neutrals, and did not fully recover with the coming of peace. The recovery of the port of Liverpool was largely fuelled by growth in other trades, including petroleum products, refrigerated goods and, above all, bulk grain. The belated completion of Gladstone Dock in 1927 enabled higher efficiencies for the liner trade and assisted recovery. From a very weak position in 1921, new record tonnage and revenue figures were posted in 1938.

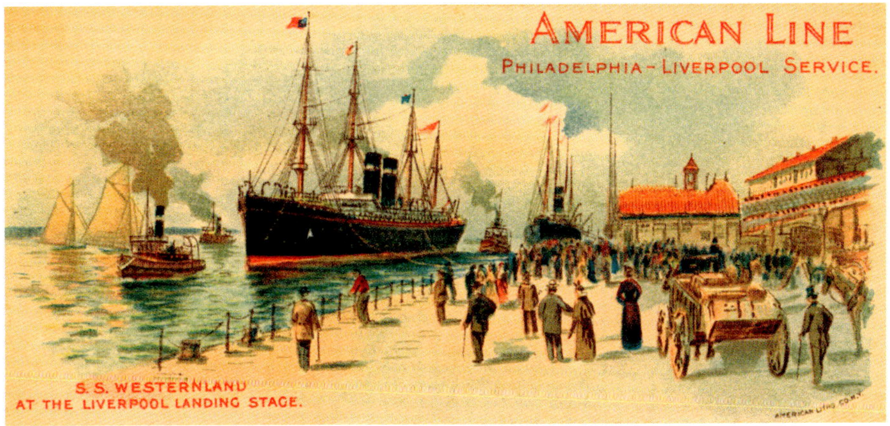

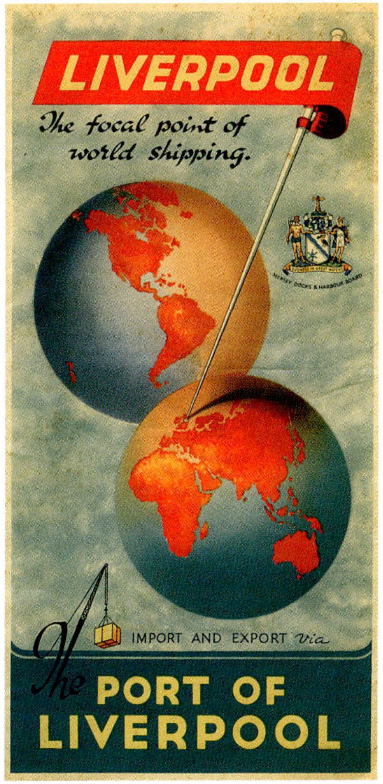

The Second World War brought similar problems to the first, with the addition of the Blitz. It has been suggested that, in relation to population, the attacks on Liverpool were the heaviest in the country: massive damage was done to the port infrastructure at a time when a great deal of expenditure was already needed to catch up on arrears of maintenance and improvement which had accumulated during the Depression. Once again the port managed to recover, in part through bulk oil tankers out-growing the Manchester Ship Canal and moving downstream to a new oil terminal at Tranmere, supplemented by a rapid growth in the importing of iron ore. A new tonnage record was set in 1964.

The 'Shipping Revolution' came to Liverpool in 1966, with the decision to construct a temporary container berth, opened in 1968 to handle the new trade while purpose-built facilities at Royal Seaforth were under construction. Unfortunately the burden of old debts, together with new ones, incurred at historically high rates of interest combined with Government vacillation to bring about the collapse of the Mersey Docks & Harbour Board. Privatisation, followed by a painful capital re-organisation, still left the Port in a weak financial position, but since 1984 business has been improving at an accelerating rate, with new record tonnages handled in recent years. At the time of writing, investment is planned for two fast-growing trades, namely cruise liners and 'post-Panamax' container ships, which will carry up to twice as many containers as the largest vessels currently using the port.

The port and its trades have changed a great deal over the years, but that is how it has always been in the port services industry: the only thing that never changes is the need to change.

Dr Adrian Jarvis

Paintings

RMS *Britannia*, 1840, Samuel Cunard's first ship, in which Charles Dickens sailed to USA in 1842

In 1837 Brunel's *Great Western* rightly became the first paddle steamer to be regarded as fast and robust enough to form the basis of a regular 'Atlantic Ferry' and three years later, Samuel Cunard's *Britannia* showed little technical catch-up.

The reason that Cunard went on to become one of the most recognisable brand names of all time, while almost no-one has heard of the Great Western Steamship Company, was that the latter pursued further engineering excellence in the shape of the astonishing *Great Britain*, which entered service in 1843. The rather more business-savvy Cunard had correctly identified the problem: neither *Great Western* nor *Britannia* could sustain a mail service on its own: instead of a wonder-ship, Cunard built the comparatively mundane *Acadia*, *Columbia* and *Caledonia*, three sisters for *Britannia* which enabled a fortnightly mail service to Boston. The contract was won and sailings begun before even the form of propulsion of *Great Britain* had been agreed by the Great Western board.

Britannia is remembered for another reason: on 3 January 1842 she took on board a passenger named Charles Dickens, who published quite an extensive account of his voyage in his *American Notes*. He was not at all impressed with the size of his 'state room' or of the saloon, or with the veracity of the person who had described them to him when selling him his ticket. The value of his reflections is diminished by the fact that *Britannia* was struck by a storm which made him feel more than a bit unwell – to the extent of staying in his cabin for four days – but his account of the vessel shipping seas which burst in through cabin skylights makes us realise that the era of the 'floating palaces' had not quite arrived. After Dickens had begun to recover and got partly used to the extreme motion of the ship, still: "The labouring of the ship in the troubled sea on this night I shall never forget. 'Will it ever be worse than this?' was a question I had often heard asked, when everything was sliding and bumping about and when it certainly did seem difficult to comprehend the possibility of anything afloat being more disturbed without toppling over and going down. But what the agitation of a steam vessel is, on a bad winter's night in the wild Atlantic, it is impossible for the most vivid imagination to conceive. To say that she is flung down on her side in the waves, with her mats dipping into them, and that, springing up again, she rolls onto the other side, until a heavy sea strikes her with the noise of a hundred great guns and hurls her back..."

In the circumstances it is perhaps understandable that his descriptions of the accommodation and catering are limited, but he makes few complaints of the latter and seems to have enjoyed good service, including plentiful supplies of brandy and water: Dickens was so good at complaining that we may interpret silence as high praise.

Sadly, after a good deal of touring around, he returned to Liverpool on a sailing packet, so we are denied the benefit of his description of a voyage on the *Britannia* or one of her sisters in more agreeable circumstances. What the published account does make clear, however, is that trans-oceanic sea travel was a pretty hairy business, and it would remain so longer that we might expect. On 10 October 1903, for example, the comparatively huge *Etruria*, with a gross tonnage almost seven times that of *Britannia*, lost a Canadian passenger, swept overboard from a deckchair up aloft near the bridge, by a freak wave. *QE2*, about eight times larger again, and fitted with modern aids like stabilisers, could still have crew hospitalised and some £2,500 worth of glass and crockery smashed in a hurricane in 1973: 50 foot waves troubled even such a giant as her.

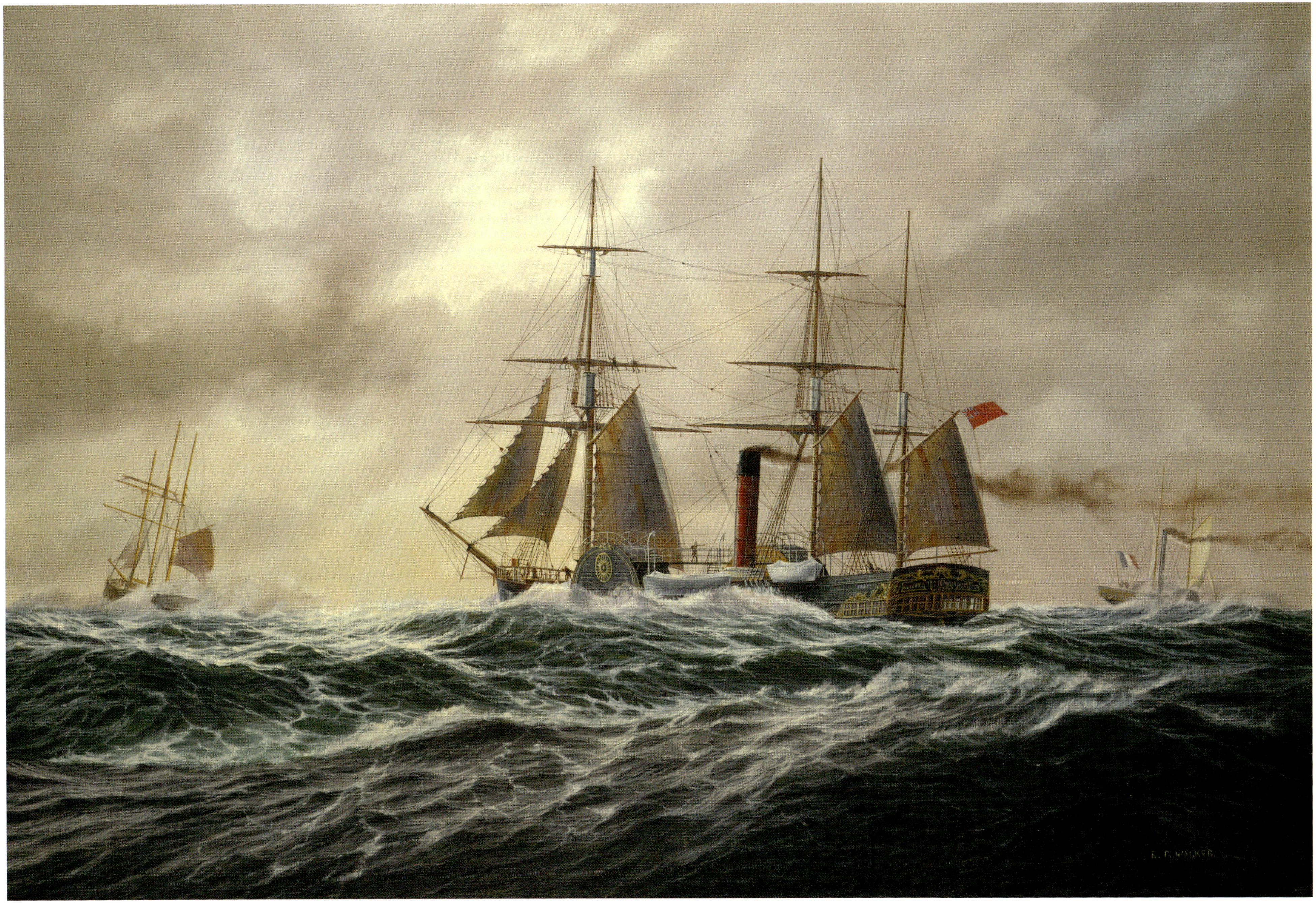

Mauretania in the Mersey, leaving for New York

In 1897 occurred an event which shook the British shipping and shipbuilding industries to the core. On her maiden voyage, Norddeutsche Lloyd's Kaiser *Wilhelm der Grosse* captured the prized 'Blue Riband of the Atlantic' from the Cunard sisterships *Campania* and *Lucania*, which had taken turns to hold it since their introduction in 1893. Worse was to come, for Hamburg-Amerika's *Deutschland* took the title briefly, only to lose it again to *Kaiser Wilhelm der Grosse's* sister *Kronprinz Wilhelm*.

It is difficult now to imagine the seriousness with which this affront was viewed by British observers of matters maritime, whether professional or amateur: the German vessels' designed 'normal speed' was a whole 0.75 knots faster than the Cunarders'. It was the natural birthright of Britons to glow with pride at the mention of the Royal Navy or of Cunard!

The response was a measured one. To make a new ship that was substantially faster than the Germans would probably be a simple matter in principle, because (Sir) Charles Parsons was British. At the Diamond Jubilee Naval Review of 1897 he turned up uninvited in his experimental steam yacht *Turbinia* and when a destroyer was sent to eject him from the party he put on full steam, leaving one of the fastest vessels in the navy for dead. But it was highly unlikely that such a fast passenger liner could pay its way in normal trading conditions: it would have heavy R&D costs, it would need to be substantially larger than any ship previously built and even with the enhanced efficiency of turbine propulsion, it was likely to consume unprecedented amounts of coal. If these money problems could be overcome it was highly likely that the British response to the technological challenge would be positively crushing. Government agreed to subsidise (by means of a low interest loan) the construction for Cunard of two vessels capable of 24-25 knots, openly referring to them as 'vessels of uneconomic speed'. As a preliminary step in their development, two modest-sized, and almost identical vessels were built, *Caronia* with reciprocating machinery and *Carmania* with turbines. The success of *Carmania* settled the matter of propulsion.

The size of the new vessels was phenomenal: *Kaiser Wilhelm der Grosse* had a gross tonnage of 14,349: *Mauretania* measured 30,696, her sister *Lusitania* very slightly less. Both comfortably exceeded 26 knots on trial – but it took 68,000 horsepower and 4,000-5,000 tons of coal per trip to do it. In September 1907 the ill-starred *Lusitania* brought the Blue Riband back where it belonged on her second voyage, only to lose it next month to *Mauretania* but regain it in November. In 1909 *Mauretania* regained it, and went on to hold it for the extraordinary total of 22 years, earning in the process the soubriquet of *'The Grand Old Lady of the Atlantic'*. She actually got faster with age, aided by improved propellors fitted in 1908 and conversion to oil-firing in 1921.

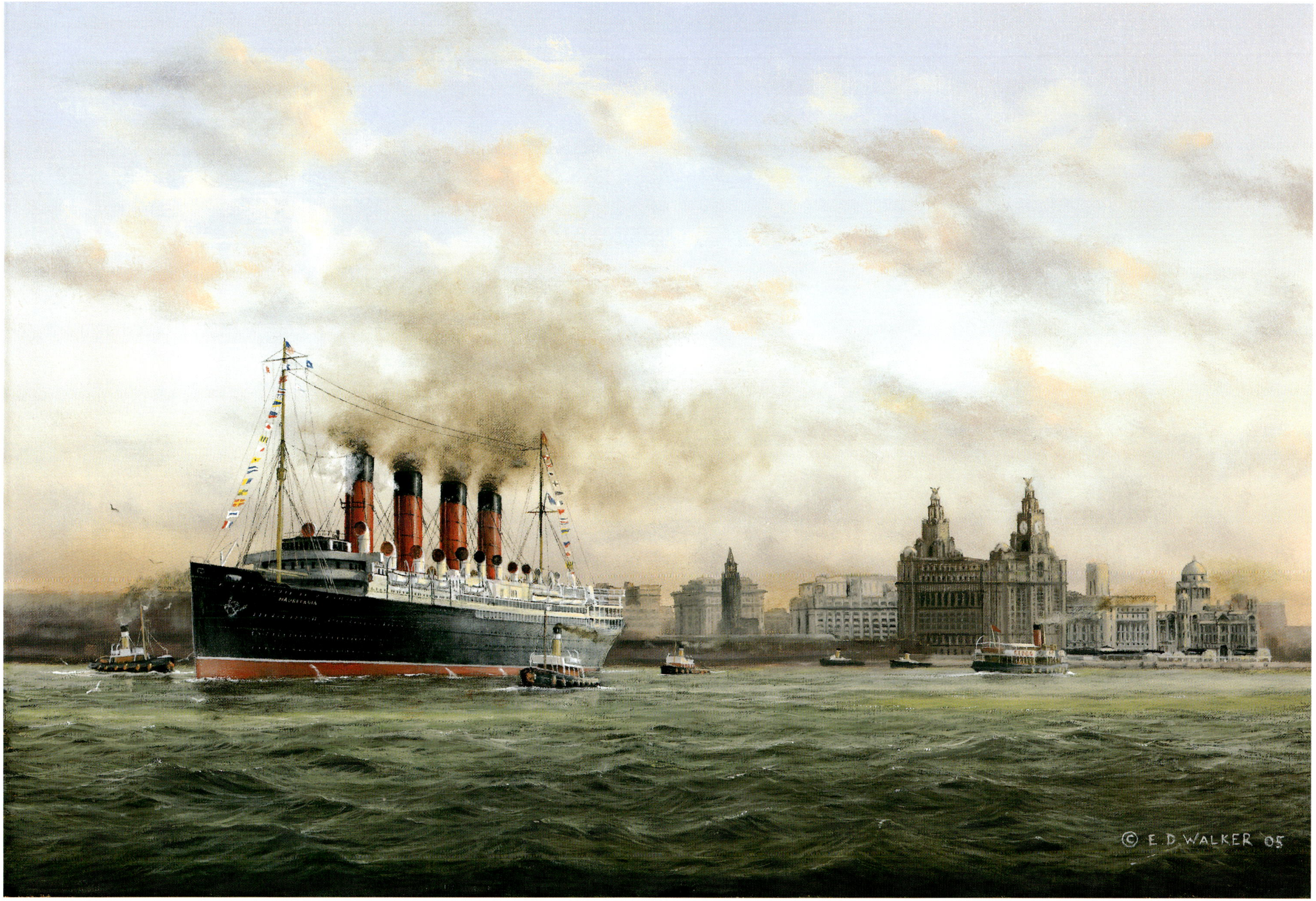
© E.D. WALKER 05

RMS *Mauretania* picking up the Pilot at Point Lynas

In this scene, one of the first generation of steam pilot boats, introduced from 1896 onwards, stands by the inward-bound *Mauretania* off Point Lynas. The small 'punt' used for actual transfer of the pilot is painted the same buff colour as the 'house funnel' of the Mersey Docks & Harbour Board. They were of very similar construction to a ship's lifeboat, but with extra strengthening and fendering to withstand the battering they suffered when trying to transfer a pilot in rough weather.

Point Lynas held an important place in the business of the port of Liverpool. It is situated a couple of miles east of the little Anglesey harbour of Amlwch, which became famous for, among other things, its exports of copper ore from Parys Mountain. As early as 1781 the Trustees of the Liverpool Docks built a lighthhouse there. But where there is a port, there are practitioners of maritime trades, which also made it suitable for a pilot station, and it gained a further feature in 1827 when the Liverpool-Holyhead semaphore telegraph replaced the earlier system of flag signalling. About one fifth of the messages it carried in 1836 related to pilotage matters, including requests back to Liverpool for a spare pilot vessel to be sent should one have to leave its station for any reason, such as putting into Amlwch for repairs.

The approaches to the Mersey had become increasingly difficult to navigate simply because the size and number of ships using them kept growing. In 1893, the Mersey Docks & Harbour Board began an attempt to dredge a large breach in the Mersey Bar which was successful in the narrow sense that it gave a much better depth of water at the bar itself, but it also changed the dynamics of the water, resulting in the formation of a 'dog leg' in the main channel to the landward side of the bar. In short, navigation became no easier and as ships continued to grow, the need for expert pilots became greater, not smaller.

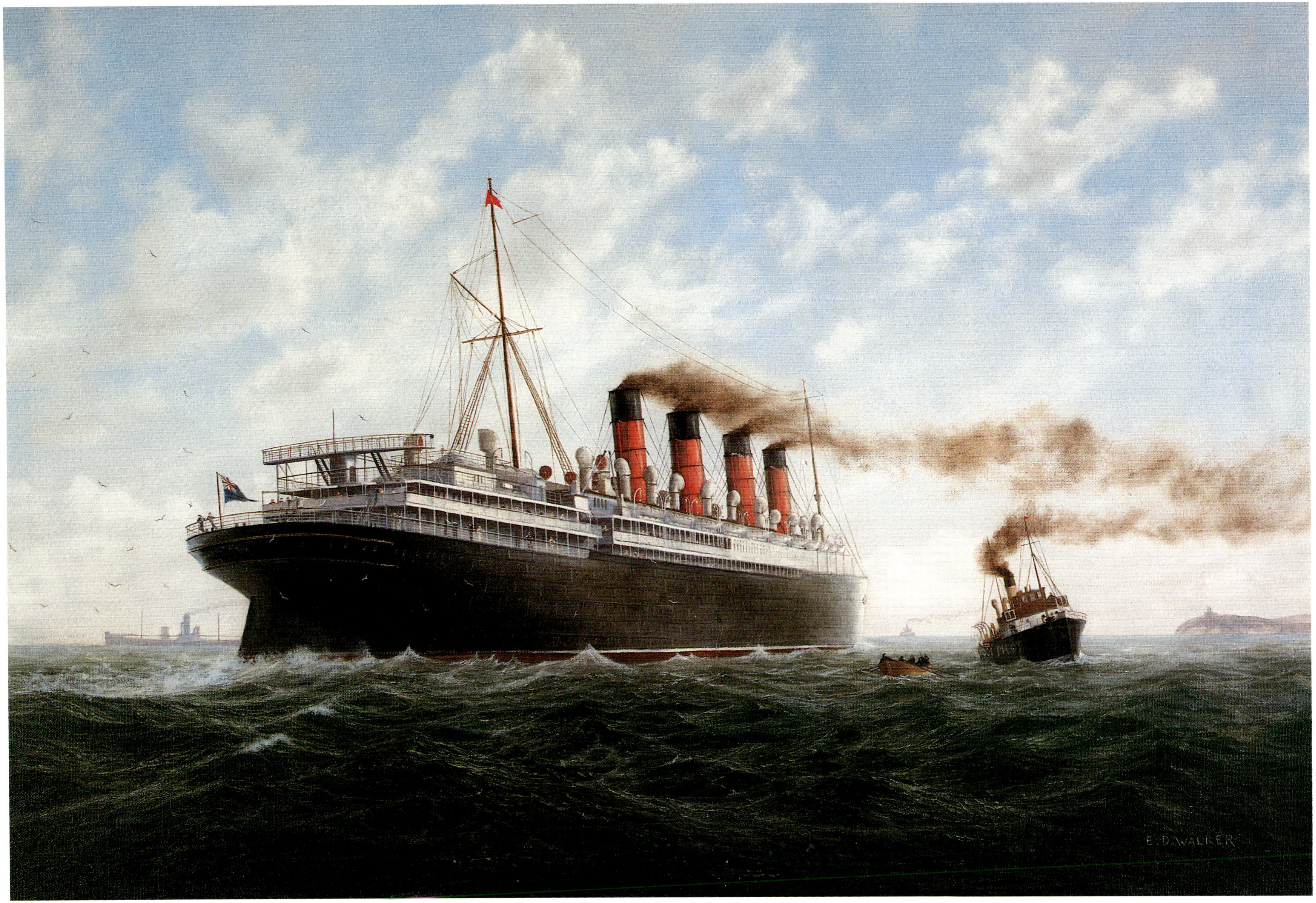
E. D. WALKER

RMS *Titanic*: The Angel of Death

The introduction of *Lusitania* and *Mauretania* may have thrown down the gauntlet most directly to Germany, but Cunard had other competitors than Hamburg-Amerika and Norddeutscher Lloyd, prominent among them the White Star Line, by then controlled by the American-led combine of International Mercantile Marine, formed in 1902. White Star's 'Big Four' (*Celtic* and sisters) were completely outclassed by the new Cunarders – indeed at 16.5 knots cruising speed they fell short on the speed of *Campania* and *Lucania* of the previous generation. When, therefore, the decision was taken to build three large liners to bring White Star back into the game, there was no intention of competing on speed: the new ships would be the largest, steadiest, most comfortable and most luxurious on the North Atlantic. Not until the Cunard Queens went into service was it possible to maintain a weekly service with only two ships, so if three ships were needed anyway, why hurry?

The new White Star liners exceeded the size of Cunard's greyhounds by near 50%, and in the interests of economy at the expense of power used a hybrid engine arrangement: the middle one of the triple screws was driven by a low-pressure turbine whose steam came from the exhaust of the largest reciprocating marine engines ever built. When, however, Cunard's team designed the *Aquitania*, which was a little larger again, they stuck with an all-turbine installation, matching White Star's luxury and still out-running them by a couple of knots.

It all sounds quite rational as a bit of shipping history, and it continued to be so as *Olympic*, the first of the three, was handed over to the owners on 31 May 1911, the same day that the second, *Titanic*, was launched. Ever since, as the subject of the greatest maritime disaster to that time, the names of her sisters have been all but forgotten and her name has become with synonymous with disaster of any kind. An attempt at reviving a flagging enterprise is routinely described as 'Re-arranging the deckchairs on the *Titanic*', implying a futile attempt to avoid inevitable destruction. What is remarkable is not that we, blessed with ninety years of hindsight, can think that way, nor is it the way in which images of the *Titanic* in literature, in all manner of commemorative material have become ubiquitous and this volume is no exception. What is remarkable is that the accident had been anticipated in a short story called 'Futility' published by Morgan Robertson in 1898. Leaving aside a few literary devices, the ways in which Robertson's fictitious liner *Titan* met its end are remarkably similar to what actually happened to *Titanic* in the small hours of 14 April 1912.

This painting reflects an incident on *Titanic's* only commercial voyage, when she anchored at Rochas Point, Queenstown, to pick up extra passengers and mails. A small black quasi-human figure appeared at the top of the aftermost funnel. Bystanders were not to know that funnels had become something of a corporate virility symbol on the North Atlantic, that No. 4 was a dummy to house ventilation uptakes and other services and for stylistic reasons, and that the tiny black figure was a stoker who had been working inside it and near the top. Thus began the story of the 'Angel of Death'. The photograph which substantiated the story may not have been printed before the ship went down…

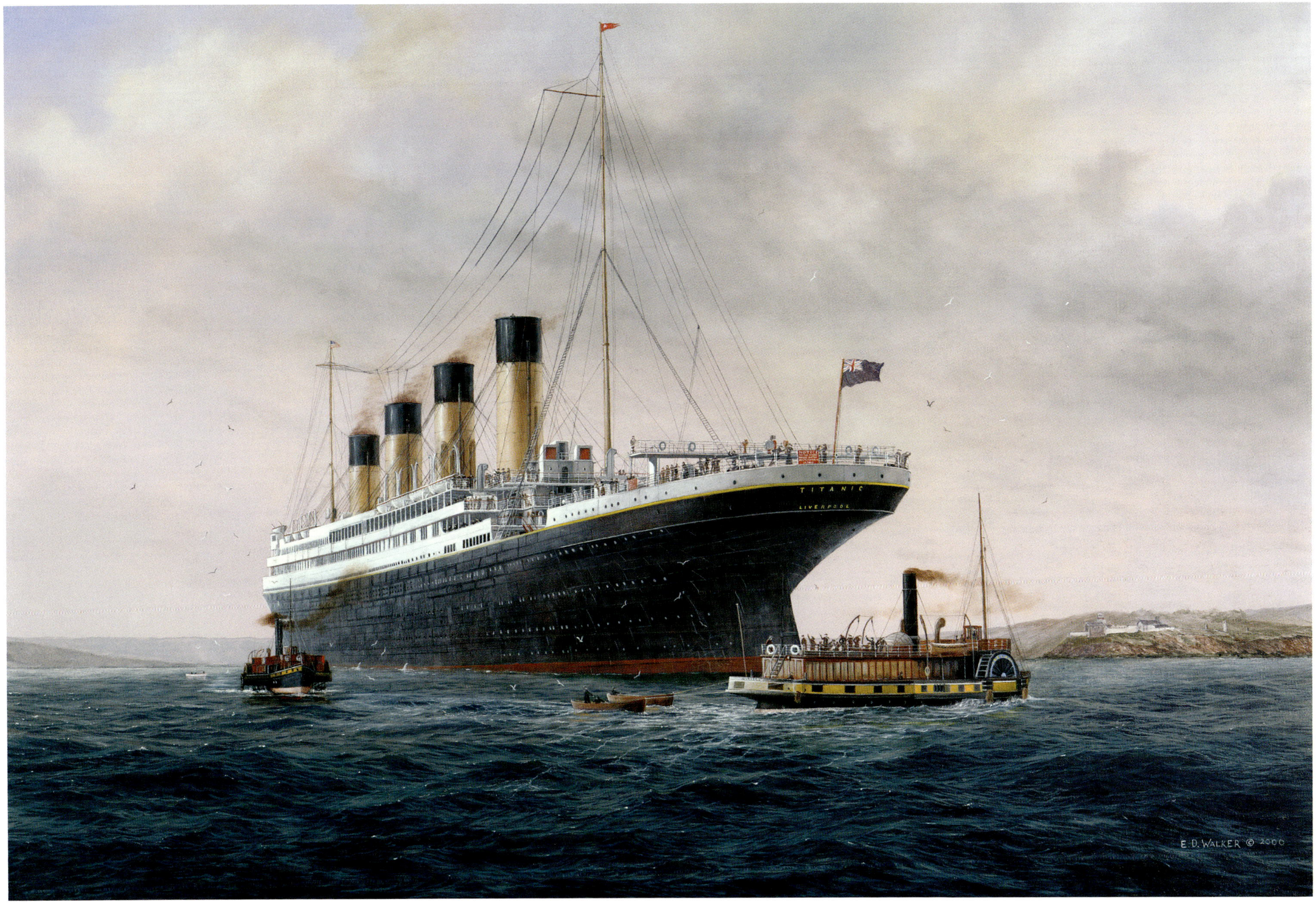
TITANIC
LIVERPOOL
E.D. WALKER © 2000

RMS *Titanic*: Pride of Ulster

Although International Mercantile Marine had been the brainchild of the American shipping magnate Clement Griscom, effective managerial control soon passed to the only one of its companies which was making any money, namely White Star. J. Bruce Ismay was elected President, and Lord Pirrie of Harland & Wolff a Board member. This guaranteed the continuation of the policy of building all White Star vessels at the Belfast yard of Harland & Wolff.

There was no reason why Ulster should not feel proud of *Olympic*'s new sister, for she was quite as splendid-looking a vessel and just as well-built and beautifully fitted out. *Olympic* was already in successful service when *Titanic* was completed, and just about the only vice she exhibited was an unduly large 'turning circle' brought about by the triple-screw arrangement. This might possibly have contributed to the disaster, as it appears that First Officer Murdock, on watch at the time, tried to steer his way out of trouble. But it was one of the many cruel ironies that night that he almost got away with it, yet it was the glancing nature of the blow which sank the ship. Had he struck the iceberg stem on, having reduced speed by what little was possible by furious reversing in the short time available, the ship would have suffered major damage, but probably survived: she was designed to remain afloat with up to three of her fifteen watertight compartments flooded: the glancing blow flooded five.

Cruel ironies and 'what if's, together with the quest for heroes and villains, have been part of the reason that funding could be found to search for the wreck and raise items from it, part, in turn, of the reason for the huge success of the film simply entitled *Titanic* after what is, with the possible exception of Noah's ark, the best-known ship's name in all history. Noah, however, landed all his passengers safely, depriving his chroniclers of the appeal peculiar to necrophilia. There was the issue of *Titanic*'s lifeboats: while totally insufficient in capacity for the number of people aboard, they exceeded the number of places required by law by well over 50%. The builders had regarded that number as insufficient but had been over-ruled by Ismay on grounds of providing uncluttered deck space for passengers to stroll - or die - on. On the other hand, although some 470 seats in the lifeboats were unoccupied, 1,503 people died, suggesting serious organisational failure at the boat stations. There were also embarrassing discrepancies in the survival rates of passengers in the different classes: First class males had a death rate of 32% while third class had 83%.

Next came the search for scapegoats. Ismay was a strong candidate by virtue of the fact he survived, and there were allegations that he had given instructions to Captain Smith which persuaded him to travel faster than was safe in the circumstances. Captain Lord, of the *Californian*, was widely vilified for not going to the rescue. He was nearer than the *Carpathia* (see page 20) but had only one radio operator and he was off watch. Various 'mystery vessels' are said by some to have been in the area. There were two enquiries, one in USA and one in Britain which came to somewhat ambiguous conclusions, leaving people plenty of scope to believe their prejudices and argue about them to this day. Perhaps the least controversial aspect of the whole tragic episode was the recognition of two further groups of heroes to join *Carpathia 's* Captain Rostron and its crew. One was the engineering staff, many of whom gave their lives to keep the generating plant going virtually to the end in order to provide light to facilitate the escape of others. The other was the band, though even there some doubt has been cast on what they were playing when the ship went down.

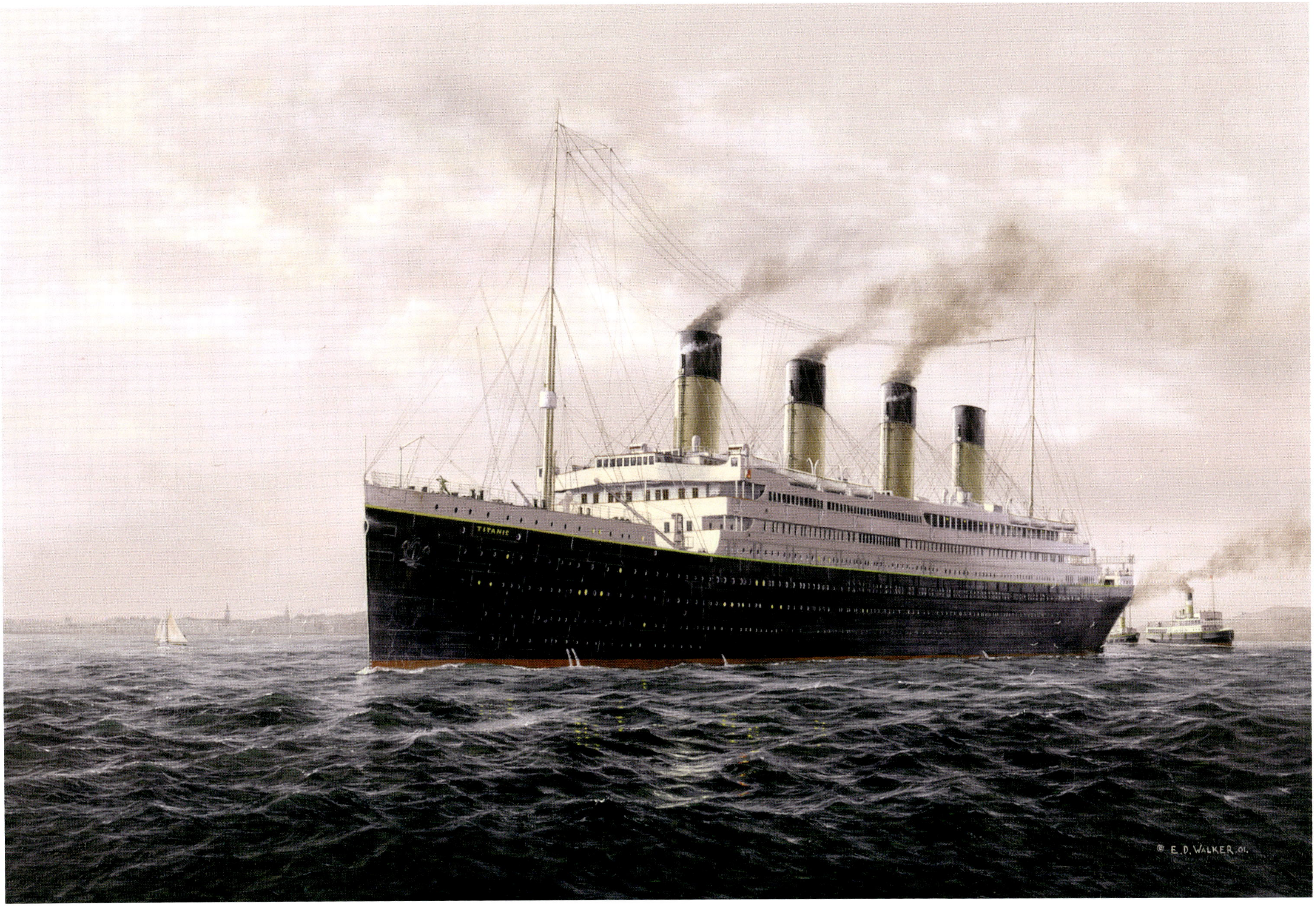
TITANIC
© E.D. WALKER. 01.

Carpathia picking up survivors of the *Titanic* disaster

Such is the glamour of the name of Cunard that we tend to forget those Cunarders which were not in contention for the Blue Riband. *Carpathia* was a distinctly second-string Cunarder which carried only second and third class passengers, initially between Liverpool and Boston, later to other American ports. Following a cruise in the Mediterranean, she began to work Cunard's Trieste – New York service. She provided third-class accommodation which set new standards on the north Atlantic, but with a designed top speed of 15 knots, an ocean greyhound she was not. Built at Swan Hunter's Newcastle yard in 1903, her quadruple expansion reciprocating engines produced a modest 9,000 indicated horsepower compared with the 68,000 of *Mauretania's* mighty turbines just four years later. But although these ships may have shared a house funnel, they were not in the same marketplace, as may be seen at a glance: *Mauretania's* four great raked stacks and two masts contrast sharply with *Carpathia's* rather tall and spindly single stack and four masts. Scores of Cunard 'slow boats', whether on the Liverpool-North America services or plying the Mediterranean, have been consigned to history's great waste paper basket, remembered only by maritime historians and shiplovers.

The event which brought this particular prosaic vessel lasting fame was the sinking of the *Titanic* in the small hours of 15 April 1912. *Carpathia's* radio operator received *Titanic's* distress call, and Captain Rostron immediately changed course to render assistance. The vessel was prepared for picking up survivors either from the water or, as Rostron would presumably have expected, from the decks of the stricken *Titanic*, and meanwhile Chief Engineer Alexander Johnstone and his men worked the engines up to 17 knots and sustained that speed for the rest of the 58 miles she had to steam to the point where *Titanic* had sunk at 2.20am. Between 4.00am when she arrived and 9.00am she picked up all of the 703 passengers and crew who survived the disaster, lifted their lifeboats aboard and, having insufficient stores to continue to his next intended port of call in the Azores with so many extra passengers, Rostron turned back and proceeded to New York.

Almost the only aspect of the whole *Titanic* story which has not been controversial in one way or another was the hero's welcome accorded to Captain Rostron (who was to be rewarded with, inter alia, the command of *Mauretania* and a knighthood) and his crew when they landed the survivors and for long afterwards. But ships cannot be kept in port for such things, and *Carpathia* sailed for Gibraltar just two days later. In 1915 she was placed on the Liverpool – New York – Boston service, where she continued until just after midnight on 17 July 1918, when she was out of Liverpool, bound for Boston. To the north west of Bishop's Rock she was torpedoed by U55, killing five of the engine room crew. The passengers and the rest of the crew, 57 in all, successfully abandoned ship and fortunately for them, the sloop HMS *Snowdrop* was nearby both to drive off the submarine and pick them up and take them back to Liverpool.

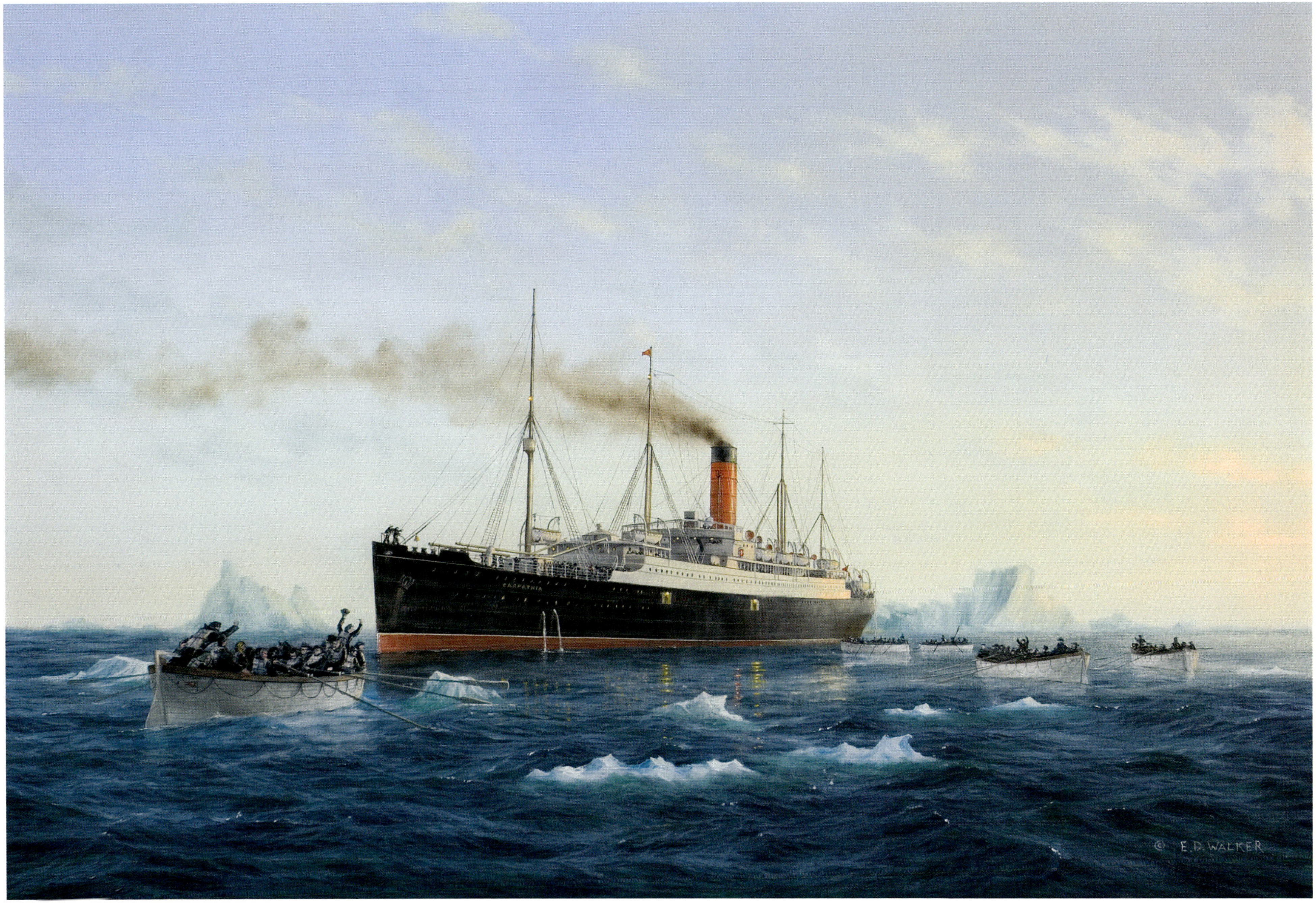
CARPATHIA
© E.D. WALKER

Aquitania leaving the Mersey

Aquitania was one of a kind for Cunard, symbolised by being the last British 'four-stacker'. She had, however, taken on the philosophy of *Titanic*, in that at 45,647 gross tons she was about 50% bigger than *Mauretania* and *Lusitania* but did not attempt to better their speed, having a 'normal speed' of 24 knots. Such was the curve of a graph of power against speed that one knot more would have required about 15,000 horsepower more, which is a lot of shovelsful of coal. She was there to compete with the luxury of *Olympic* and *Britannic* rather than with the 'greyhounds' and despite her much larger size she had only a little over 85% of their power.

The absurd lengths to which competition on the North Atlantic went may perhaps be appreciated by the little story of the Hamburg-Amerika liner *Imperator*, which had been designed to be the biggest ship in the world. Its length overall was found to be smaller than that of the incomplete *Aquitania*, so a huge and entirely superfluous Imperial Eagle was added as a sort of latter-day figurehead. This reputedly suffered a certain amount of storm damage, but be that as it may; it had been removed in 1913, making Aquitania officially what all true-born Britons knew all along that she was, namely the biggest as well as the best, ship in the world.

She had a brief and abortive career as an armed merchant cruiser – a role for which she was totally unsuited and which served only to clog up the Port of Liverpool's best transit shed (at Gladstone Graving Dock) with all her discarded furniture and fittings when it should have been full of war supplies. And splendours they were, as surviving photographs show: the opulent Carolean Smoking Room would bring tears to the eyes of present-day smokers who, huddled on office doorsteps, add deaths from hypothermia to the statistics for other 'smoking-related diseases'. It took a while for anyone to find any use for her, and when they did it was as a troop transport to Mudros to support the disastrous Gallipoli landings.

The rest of her Great War career is confused, confusing and really rather unedifying. At one stage she was discharged from Government service, but soon afterwards was converted (again) into a hospital ship. The simple fact is that everybody knew that such a large fast vessel must be immensely useful for something – but for what?

Then came a captive market of passengers – US troops. Even better, the survivors needed to get home at the end of the war. *Aquitania* was busy like never before but how long could it last?

Aquitania just went on and on. She was converted to oil firing and in 1920 went back into regular transatlantic service, in which she continued, with a few deviations into pleasure cruising, until war broke out again. She served in a variety of relatively unimportant capacities until the time of mass troop movements arrived again, but she was also involved in some large-scale emergency evacuations.

There's no such thing as gratitude to old ships, however great our debt to them. *Aquitania* served with honour through two world wars and those things which went wrong, mostly went wrong through government interference or incompetence, but with the two 'Queens' able to maintain the weekly Southampton-New York sailings on their own, there was no role for *Aquitania*, and she went to the breaker's' yard in 1949.

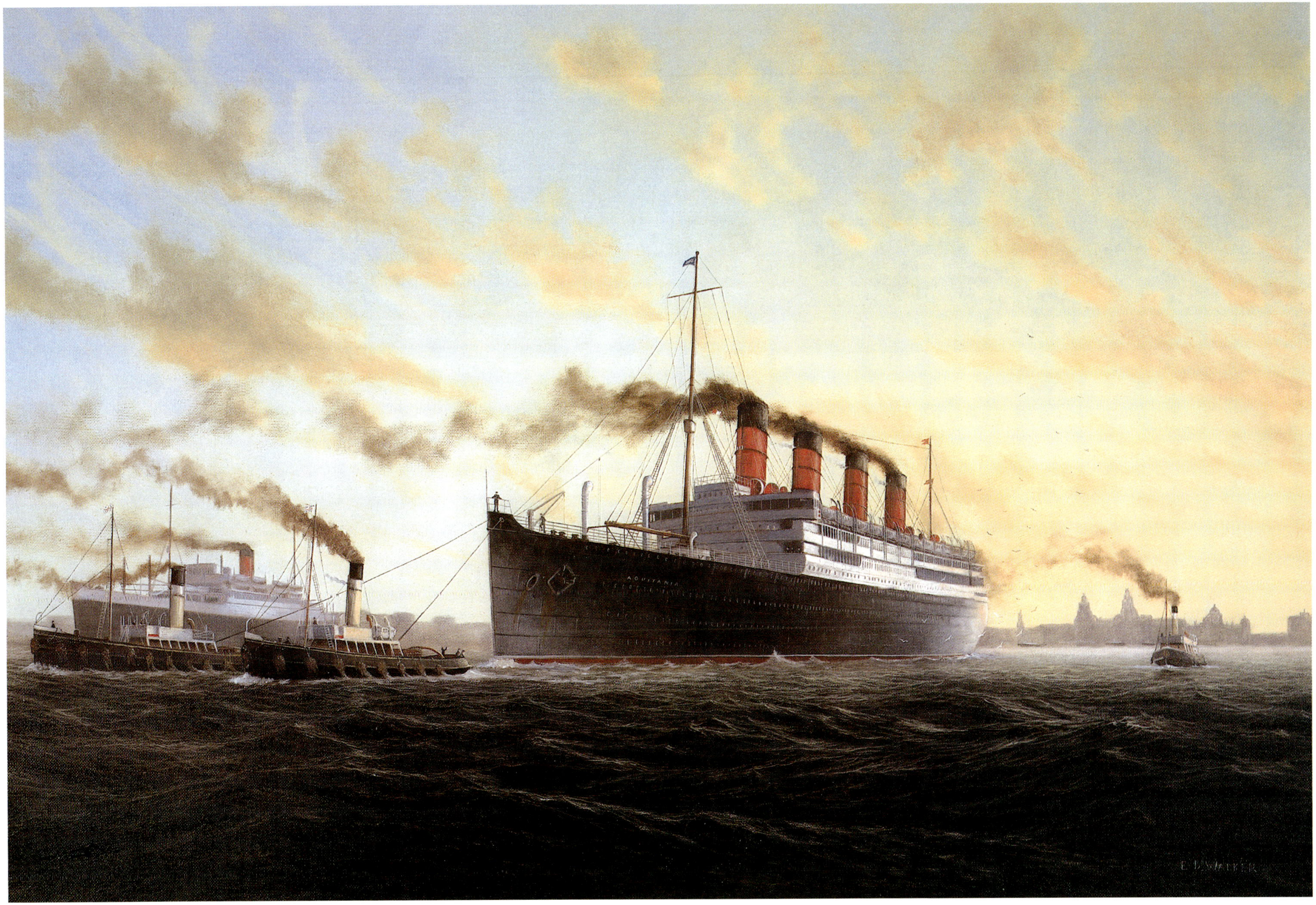

White Star Liner *Celtic* aground at Rochas Point, Ireland

Celtic was one one the so-called 'Big Four' White Star liners, and at the time of her launch in 1901 was the largest ship in the world, remaining so until the arrival of *Lusitania* and *Mauretania* in 1907. All four were built on the principle of providing size, (20,880 gross tons), spaciousness, comfort and reasonably high speed (16 knots) without spending huge sums in the pursuit of the Blue Riband. This was, of course, the design philosophy continued in *Titanic* and her sisters. Although the 'Big Four' were considered express liners, they did carry a relatively large proportion of third class. Their capacity of 2,350 was almost five times as many as first and second classes together.

Titanic became famous for being lost, but she was only the biggest entry in the catalogue of death and destruction which is the history of the White Star line. Some of their more avoidable disasters involved colliding with immovable objects, such as Marr's Head in the case of *Atlantic* or Ireland in the case of *Celtic*. Until this accident, she had been, by White Star standards, a fairly lucky ship, having suffered only a couple of minor cotton cargo fires in 1906 and 1909 and a fairly trivial collision in the Mersey in 1903. In the small hours of 10 December 1928, attempting to enter Cobh harbour to land the mails and 70 passengers, she was caught in bad and deteriorating weather which prevented the pilot getting aboard. Captain Berry moved slowly towards the harbour, but at about 4.45am she grounded, initially undramatically, on the Cow and Calf rocks. He gave the order to abandon ship, but once passengers were at boat stations, decided that as the tide was falling there was no immediate danger and passengers were able to have breakfast before being tendered ashore in a pretty laid-back manner.

The painting conveys the misplaced confidence everyone seems initially to have shared in refloating her and towing her off to be repaired. Tugs arrived, followed by two Liverpool & Glasgow Salvage Association vessels with powerful pumps and the equipment and materials for constructing cofferdams. But a survey by their divers revealed that the sea had been bumping her up and down on the rocks, causing extensive damage and a few days later it was decided that repair was impossible and she must be broken up where she lay, work which took some four years to complete.

If there is any consolation in this sorry tale, it is that previous disasters, both in peace and in war, had so focussed attention on the mechanics of evacuation and rescue that in this instance everybody, down to and including the ship's cats, got safely ashore.

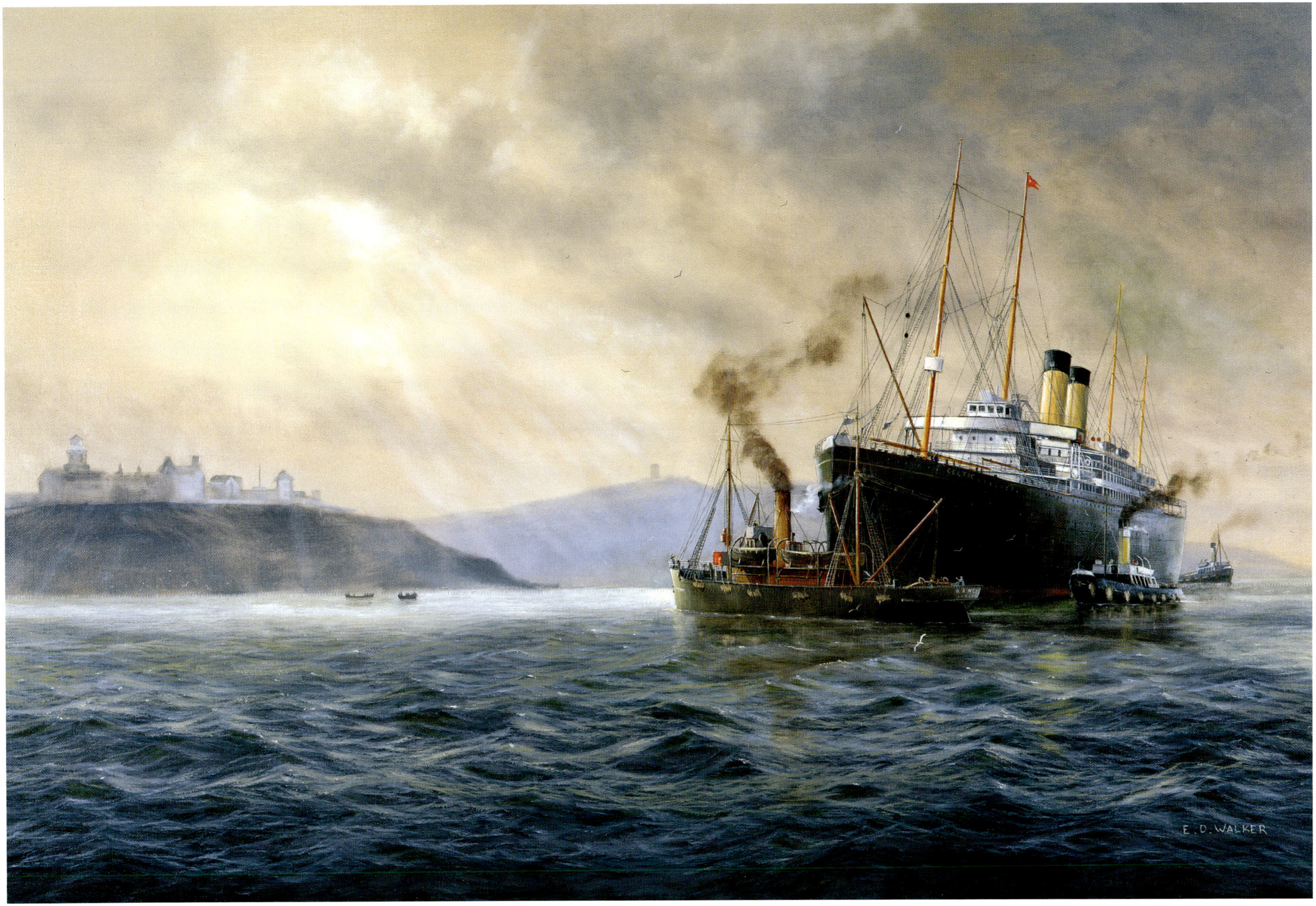
E. D. WALKER

Franconia in the Mersey

At the end of the Great War, Cunard was left needing not only to replace significant war losses but also to catch up on creeping obsolescence in its fleet, which continues in war as it does in peace. The result was a considerable building programme which included *Albania, Scythia, Samaria, Laconia, Tyrrenia, Lancastria, Andania, Antonia,* and *Ausonia* in the years 1920-22, not to mention the refitting of the Hamburg-Amerika Line's *Imperator*, handed to Cunard as 'reparation' for the sinking of the *Lusitania* and duly re-named *Berengaria*.

Commissioned in June 1923, *Franconia* was a comparatively modest 'slow boat', intended for the Liverpool – New York Service, but at the stately and economical speed of 16 knots, which left her a long way in the wake of the sixteen-year-old *Mauretania*, still racing across the North Atlantic at 25+ knots but using a lot of oil in the process.

Franconia measured 20,175 gross tons and was 625ft long by 77ft 3in wide. Her twin double reduction turbines produced a mere 13,500 shp compared with *Mauretania's* 68,000. She still had a clear eye to the fast-disappearing emigrant traffic, as her third class passenger capacity was almost double that of first and second together, yet within her first year of operation was engaged in cruising, which seems to have been her main activity, both for Cunard and for Furness Bermuda Line, to whom she was chartered 1931-32. It has been suggested that she was an elegant ship, and perhaps within her class she was. But her prominent cargo-handling areas both fore and aft breach the pre-Great War social dictate that one should never be aware of what the servants are doing. In those terms, she is an ugly ship. But she continued as a successful cruise vessel.

She had a generally successful time in the second world war as well, apart from an embarrassing collision with the Royal Mail Lines' *Alcantara* in October 1939. She gained rather more than 15 minutes of fame by serving as the headquarters of the British delegation to the Conference of Yalta. But having been re-fitted to go back into passenger service, she grounded her stern while leaving Quebec, which put her out of action for eight weeks and this was followed by various mechanical failures: she had been a good ship, but she was past it now and in December 1956 she made her last voyage to the breaker's yard.

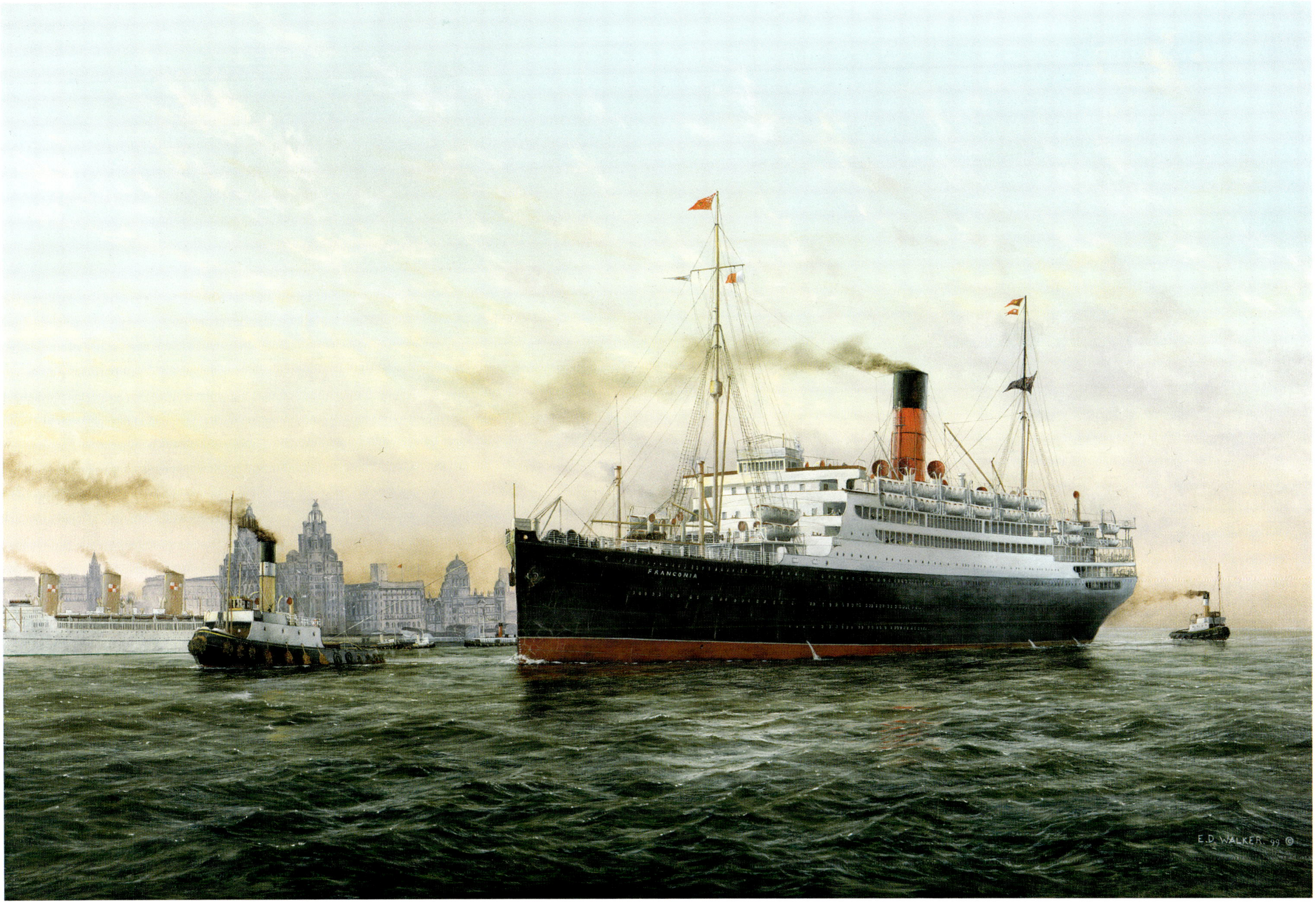
FRANCONIA
E.D. WALKER 99 ©

Reina del Pacifico

In the 1820s it seems to have been commonly believed in Britain that to get rich it was only necessary to head for South America with a shovel and wheelbarrow, with which to remove as much precious metal as you could trundle back to a ship. At one remove, Latin American government bonds were an infallible path to wealth beyond the dreams…of reasonable expectation. Speculative booms brought shipping bubbles in their wake, but by 1840, when the Pacific Steam Navigation Company got its charter, things were getting a little saner.

What lay behind its establishment was not so much the imagination of Eldorado as the recognition that in addition to trading between Europe and Latin America, it was possible to operate profitable long-distance coastal services around central and south America because inland transport, whether north/south or east/west was distinctly poor. This situation would change as large amounts of railway materials and machinery were shipped there from Britain, but it did not change quickly. PSNC, from the beginning, served a wide variety of destinations from the West Indies round the Horn to Chile. They dabbled in the Australia trade as well. But wherever goods went, merchants and agents wanted to go too, to keep an eye on their business. There was a demand for passenger as well as cargo carriage.

Reina del Pacifico was almost the last of the line. Built in 1931 by Harland & Wolff, she could have been cancelled (the order was at one stage suspended) as a result of the collapse of Royal Mail Lines, which had taken over PSNC, in 1930. Happily, PSNC was 'de-merged', leaving *Reina del Pacifico* unscathed. Like other ships on Southern Hemisphere routes she was both small and slow compared with the 'ocean greyhounds': a mere 574 ft long by 76.4 ft wide and measuring 17,872 gross tons. She was propelled by four diesel engines by Harland and Wolff and had a maximum speed of 18 knots. A typical voyage might be Liverpool to Valparaiso via Bermuda and the Panama Canal, with calls at other intermediate ports, which would take 27 days. She served as a troopship throughout World War 2 and was not released until 1946, after which re-fitting for passenger use took two years.

Up to this point she had been regarded as a lucky ship, but her luck turned when she was on re-commissioning trials: an engine-room explosion killed 28 men and delayed her return to service by another six months. In July 1957 she ran aground on Devil's Flat, Bermuda and on her very next voyage she suffered serious trouble with her generating plant. Demand for berths had been falling and the larger and more modern *Reina del Mar* (built 1956) could maintain the service on her own, so in 1958 *Reina del Pacifico* was sold and broken up in Newport, South Wales. *Reina del Mar* was withdrawn in 1963, chartered for cruising and finally broken up in Taiwan in 1975. She was PSNC's last vessel.

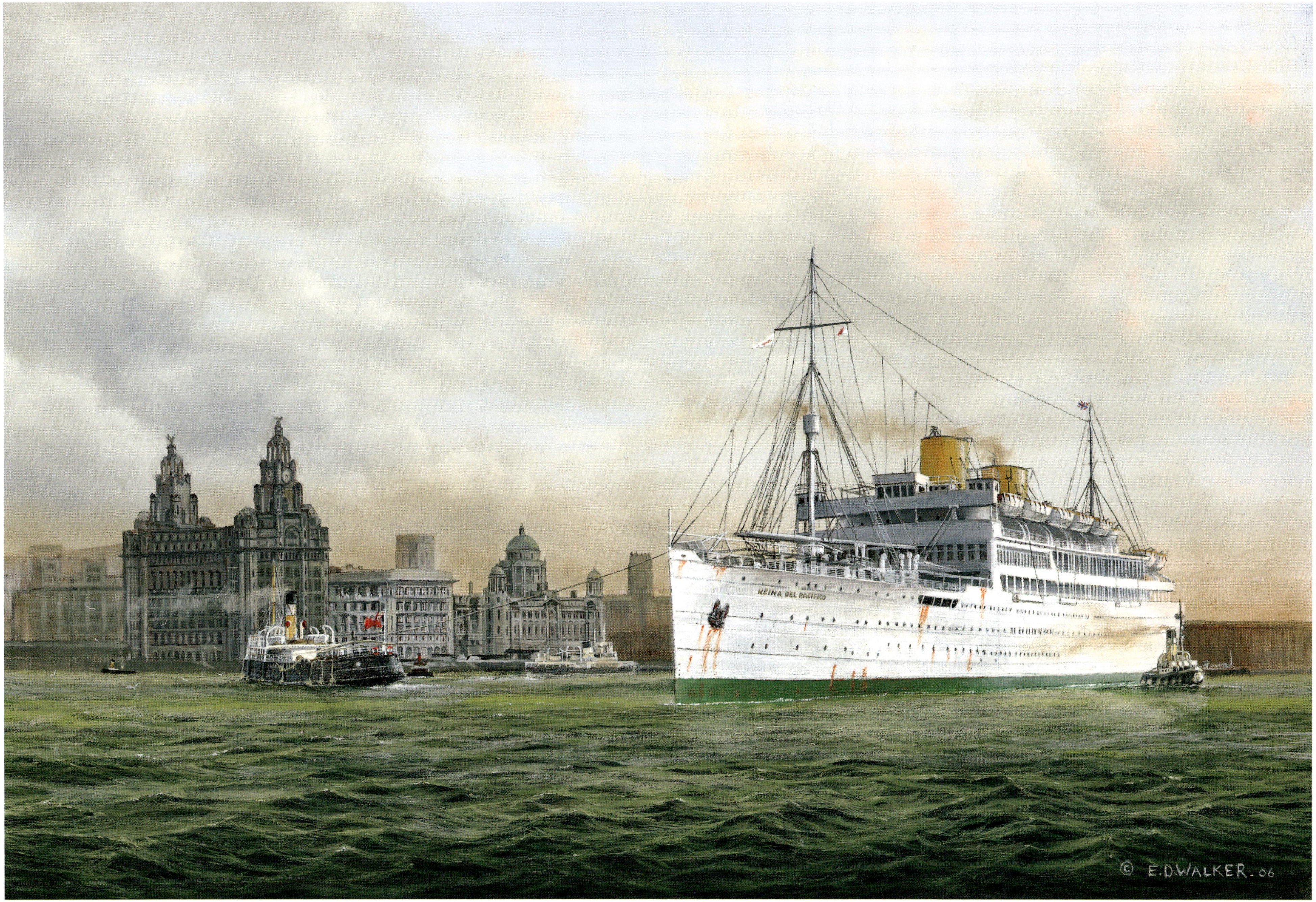
© E.D.WALKER.06

Saxonia in the Mersey

Saxonia was the first of the quartet which included *Sylvania*, which appears in the background of the painting on page 89. The other two were *Ivernia* and *Carinthia*. They were built to replace the tired and elderly *Franconia* and her near-sisters *Scythia* and *Samaria* on the Montreal route, based on a decision of 1951, but the last of them, *Sylvania*, did not actually enter service until 1957. They cost a total of £21,000,000 to build, and given the rapid growth of airline traffic at the time one wonders how well spent that money was. The ships did at least have the advantage that they had been designed with the emigrant traffic very much in mind, with a tourist: 1st Class ratio of over 6:1. Air might be fast, but it was not yet cheap.

They were, by Cunard standards at the time, fairly small vessels, with gross tonnages varying slightly around 22,500. Their overall length was 608 feet and breadth 80ft 3in and their 24,500 shp steam turbines were designed to drive them at the very reasonable speed (for vessels carrying emigrants on assisted passages) of 20 knots. In fact, *Saxonia* set a new record for the Montreal trip on her maiden voyage, actually averaging rather more than that throughout. Despite her relatively humble role in the Cunard scheme of things, *Saxonia* was the first of their ships to be fitted with active stabilisers. She and her sisters were all built by John Brown & Co, and, alone among Cunarders, had the distinctive 'domed' top to her comparatively stumpy raked single funnel. She was a well-balanced looking ship, with a moderate superstructure and four derricks both fore and aft.

In 1962, Cunard decided that their heavy trading losses could best be cut by fitting out *Saxonia* and *Ivernia* as cruise liners, at a cost of £12,000,000. On the one hand they were given modern features like air conditioning, while on the other the nostalgia card was played by re-naming them *Carmania* and *Franconia*. Their 'newness' was announced to the world by their hulls being painted pale green, though, of course, the traditional Cunard funnel colours were retained.

But these were grim times for Cunard. The new cruising sisters encountered labour, engineering and safety problems but were still capable of losing money unaided by outside factors, and in 1971 they were withdrawn from service and laid up. In 1973, a complex purchase arrangement saw *Carmania* (née *Saxonia*) re-named again as *Leonid Sobinov*, of the Soviet Union merchant service, which apparently operated her both as a passenger liner and as a cruise ship out of Sydney. By this time, of course, Cunard had severed all its connections with Liverpool, including the sale of the magnificent Cunard Building at the Pier Head, except for its involvement in Atlantic Container Lines. It is to be hoped that the connection will be revived.

The vessel at the Stage is Elder Dempster's TSMV *Apapa*, a typical passenger and cargo liner for the West Africa trade, built in 1948, while in the background are *Manxman* (see page 86) and a P-class Blue Funnel liner (see page 42).

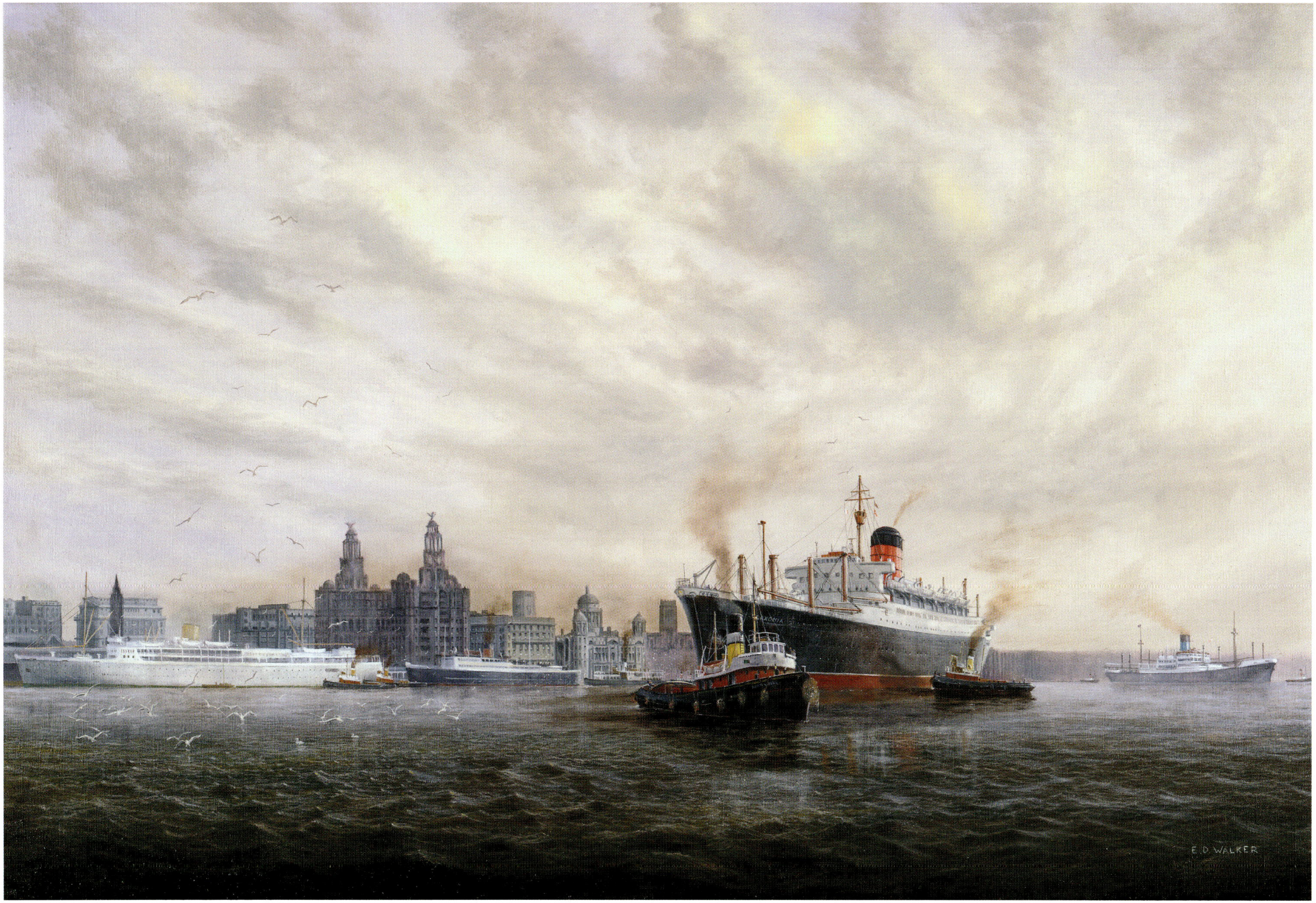
E.D. WALKER

Caronia in the Mersey

This is the third ship of the Cunard line to be named *Caronia*. The first (1904-32) was the one used in the great engine trial mentioned on page 14, while the second had a rather short and unhappy life (1949-67), being wrecked in Guam in 1974 while on the way to a Taiwan breaker's yard following six years' assorted ownership, spasmodic and unsuccessful operation, and litigation.

The keel of the third ship, the one shown in the painting, was laid at Swan Hunter's yard at Newcastle and represented the last major passenger order undertaken in Britain. The vessel was delivered on 17 May 1973, with a gross tonnage of 24,292, 629ft long and 82 ft wide. Her twin diesel engines of 12,000 bhp (each) sufficed for a cruising speed of 20 knots and she was to have a crew of 390.

But that delivery was not made to Cunard: the vessel was named Vistafjord and it was built for Norwegian American Cruises. Cunard only bought her in 1983. What *Caronia* was doing in Liverpool on this occasion was attending her re-naming ceremony on Friday 10 December 1999, following a refit and a 're-branding'. It was some party, with a round-Britain cruise, and lavish hospitality along the way. Liverpool puts on some good fireworks displays from time to time, but this one was a bit special.

One might wonder why Cunard chose the name, which might be associated with the obsolete technology of *Caronia I* or the misfortunes of *Caronia II*. The answer appears to be that during her time with Cunard, *Caronia II* became one of those vessels which passengers took to their hearts. It may have been because she was Cunard's first 100% cruiseliner, it may have been her distinctive green hull. Who knows? Whatever it was, it worked.

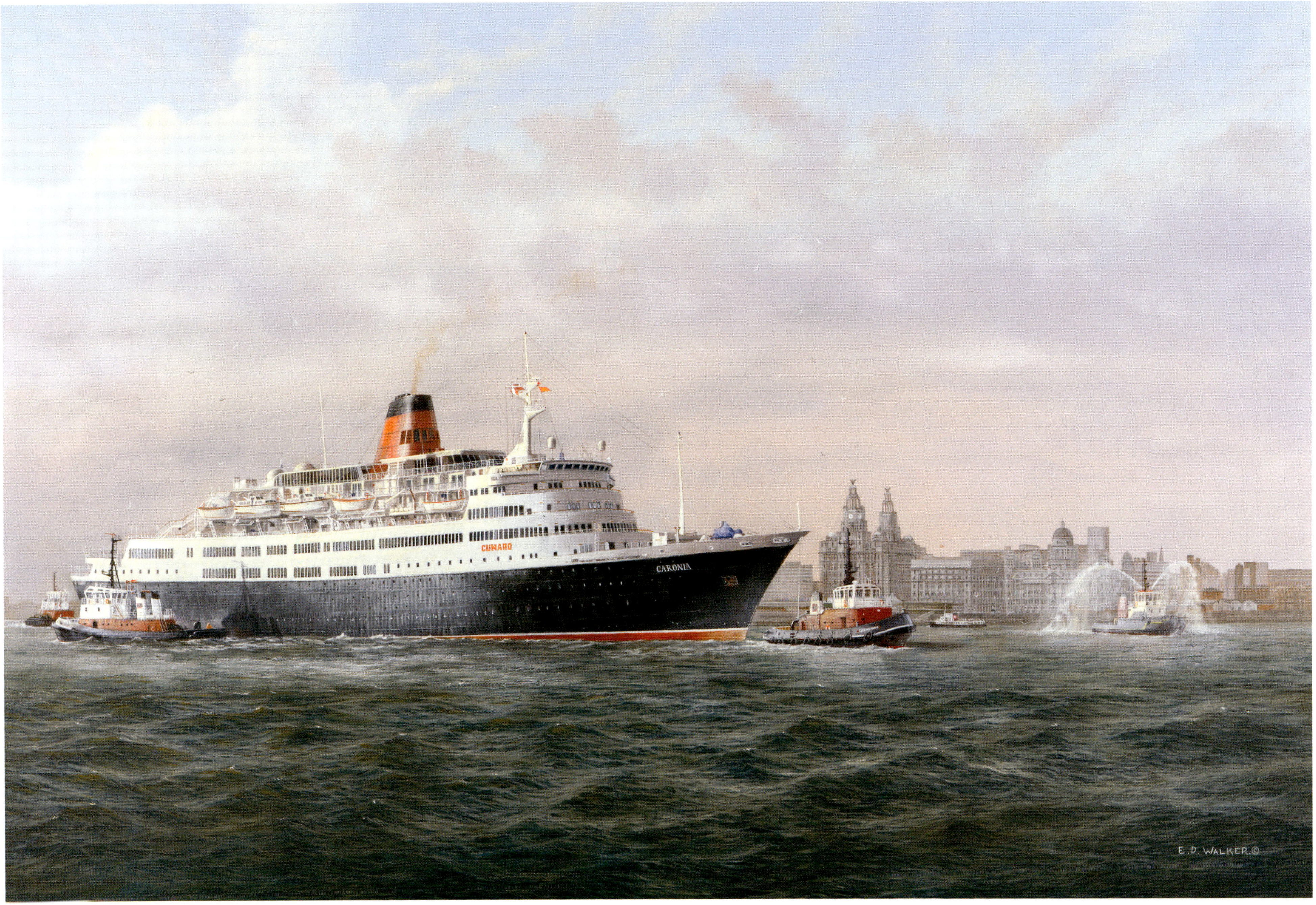
CUNARD
CARONIA
E.D. WALKER ©

QE2 in the Mersey, 25th Anniversary Cruise, 1994

The deployment of ocean-going passenger liners on pleasure cruises during the winter had its roots in the nineteenth century, but the North Atlantic Ferry was different: this was, at least for the business travellers who used the express liners, an all year round service. When, therefore, Cunard began to think about a replacement for the ageing *Queen Mary*, out-paced by some three knots by the *United States* and losing money for the company, the initial assumption was that *Q3*, as the project was dubbed, would be pretty much a single-purpose machine, like the Queens, and just as big. As *United State*s had shown, it was possible to go fast and in comfort on much less than the Queens' tonnage. More to the point, the plans for *Q3* were made public in 1961, five years after the number of trans-Atlantic air passengers first exceeded those travelling by sea. Cunard themselves were hedging their bets by investing in air travel, first in Cunard-Eagle and then Cunard-BOAC The new ship might still have a niche market among those frightened of flying, but in the winter among those prone to mal de mer…? No: this must be a dual purpose ship, equally capable of a reasonably fast Atlantic crossing or of holiday cruising.

The design adopted was both radical and commonsensical. The most obvious differences from the previous Queens were smaller size (963 feet long against the 1,031 of *Queen Elizabeth* and seven decks compared with ten) to allow passage of the Panama Canal, and the abolition of the multiple array of huge funnels which had emphasised the power and speed of Cunard's express liners since the days of *Lucania* (1893). Down below, she still had a powerful (88.000 kw, about 110,000 shp) steam turbine installation but with a 'normal speed' of 28.5 knots as against 29 in *Queen Elizabeth* and 30 in *Queen Mary*. Clearly no head-to-head with the *United States* for the Blue Riband was envisaged. Her maximum on trials was 32.66. Below the waterline were some significant changes: *QE2* was the largest twin screw vessel to date, saving the complication of four sets of machinery. She also had a bulbous bow, bow thrusters and active stabilisers fitted.

Internally, her styling was remorselessly contemporary, and it was said that the only wood used was the butchers' blocks in the galleys. The rationalisation of the number of different galleys (and hence the distances walked by waiters) was one just one among many factors which allowed an increase of the passenger:crew ratio from 1:8 in *QE* to 2:8 in *QE2*. She had one quarter the number of engineer officers and used slightly less than half as much fuel.

Final acceptance trials were geared to a handover on 1 January 1969, but damage to the blades of the main turbines meant remedial work, including a partial re-design of the blades. Her maiden voyage did not occur until 2 May 1969, but once she was fully up and running there was a good deal of optimism that her dual-role design would at least delay, if not prevent, the demise of the great passenger ship. In the event it would see it into the next century: for her further career, see overleaf.

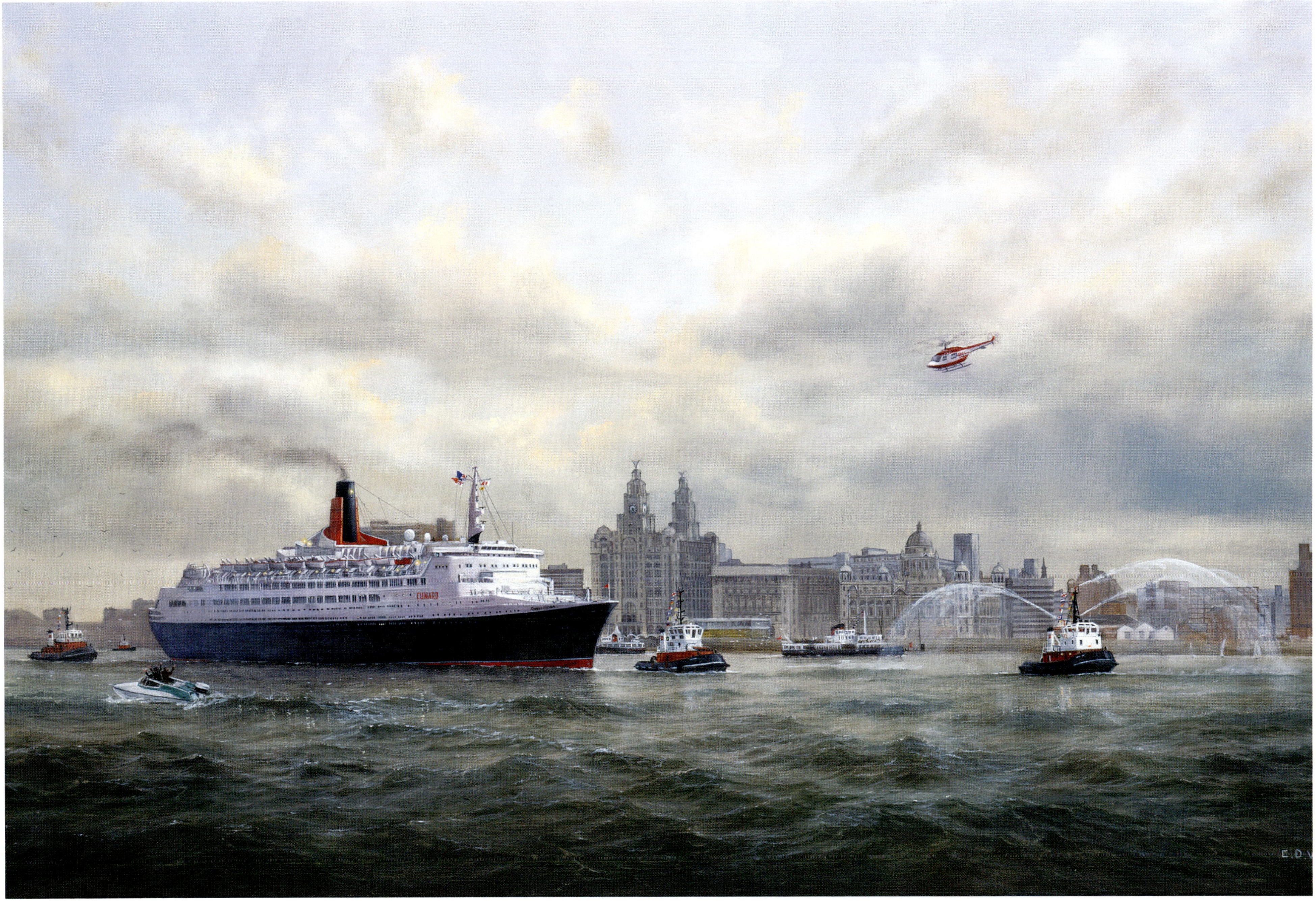

QE2 in the Mersey

The painting depicts *QE2*'s visit to Liverpool to commemorate the ship's thirtieth anniversary in 1999. Comparatively few of the great passenger liners of the past lasted so long in the front-line service of their owners. *Mauretania* (1) the 'Grand Old Lady of the Atlantic' did not quite make it, and *Aquitania* while her White Star competitor *Olympic* (sister of *Titanic*, popularly dubbed 'Old Reliable') did, but not by much. *QE2* did not at first look like competing with her giant forebears, and yet she did so and has outlasted most of them.

Her building was the usual story of delays and overspends, of government subsidies and of shipyard labour disputes which have come to characterise the history of British post-war shipbuilding. Jokes were made about her sister ship – the one built with pilfered materials which 'walked out of the gate'. Her acceptance trials in late December 1969 were unsuccessful, with Cunard refusing to accept the vessel on account of serious deficiencies in the main turbines. On investigation it was found that blades had failed on both rotors, necessitating not merely replacement but what engineers euphemistically call 'retro-fitting' – ie partial re-design. She finally set off for her maiden voyage to New York on 2 May 1969: her original maiden voyage was to have been a Christmas charity cruise. However, once into service, she had a good summer.

Her career has not been lacking in excitement: in 1972, the threat of a bomb aboard led to a bomb disposal squad being parachuted into the sea alongside her to search for it. Two years later, a problem with her boiler feedwater left her dead in the water needing to be towed to Bermuda for repairs. In 1982 she carried the Fifth Infantry Brigade to the Falklands, arriving back in Southampton on 11 June and going immediately for 're-conversion' for normal business.

In 1986 she was at the centre of outraged comment in the popular press when Cunard decided to re-engine her with diesel-electric units, which, it was estimated at the time, would save £12 million per year on fuel. What was outrageous about that? The new engines were built by MAN, and the £100 million contract for supplying and fitting them, together with new propellors and some quite extensive interior alterations went to Lloyd Werfte of Bremerhaven. The intended 'normal' speed with the new engines and propellors was unchanged as 28.5 knots, but on her speed trials she recorded 33.1 prior to her return to service in April 1887.

What's in a name?

On the occasion depicted in the painting, as on several other visits *QE2* has made to Liverpool, she caused considerable traffic congestion through people simply wanting to get to the riverfront to see her. Why? She was not built on the Mersey, nor is she Liverpool-registered. The company that owns her was planning its final removal from Liverpool at the time she went into service, and she is only an occasional visitor when cruising. While the large number of officers who have served on her over the years has included many who were Merseysiders or Merseyside trained, the majority of her crew have had no ties here.

Perhaps, if we compare the disgruntlement felt at her refitting going to Germany with that occasioned by *Kaiser Wilhelm der Grosse* gaining the Blue Riband all those years ago we might find a clue. The Cunard name was uniquely British in the palmy days of the 'Atlantic Ferry' and it remains so even when not much survives except the memory. *QE2* preserves that memory in a very real way, and everybody knows that Liverpudlians are suckers for nostalgia.

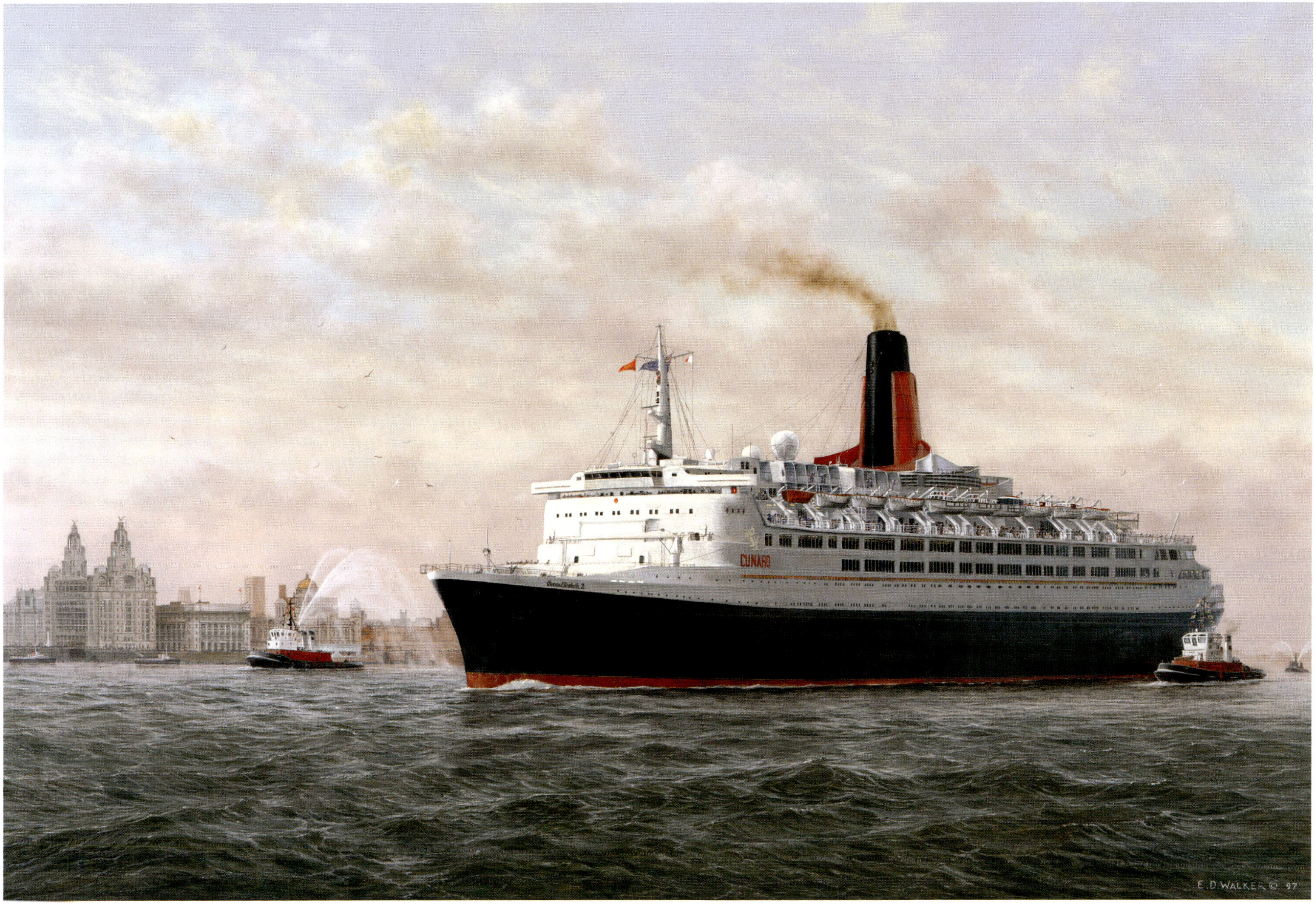
CUNARD
E.D WALKER © 97

Queen Mary 2, off Southampton

Queen Mary 2 is something few people could have imagined in, say, 1980, that they would ever see again. She is the largest passenger vessel ever built, but she is not exclusively employed in cruising: she is a true dual-purpose ship in the same way that *QE2* is, and currently makes 16 'Transatlantic Ferry' voyages per year.

She was built at Chantiers de l'Atlantique, St Nazaire, where work began in January 2002, and she was floated out of her building dock in March 2003. She went for her first sea trials in September, and despite the need for some minor re-design of the propulsion 'pods', was handed over on time in December and began her maiden voyage to Fort Lauderdale on 12 January 2004, an astonishingly short time for the construction of a vessel of huge size and unexampled complexity. This was achieved partly through the builder's capability in assembling very large pre-fabricated sections which were then craned into place, but partly also through the amount of planning that had gone into everything, not least the logistics, before anyone started cutting up metal.

The ship bristles with 'firsts' and superlatives, including a length of 345 metres (1,152 feet) and a GRT of 150,000: the corresponding figures for the old *Queen Mary* were 1,019 ft and 81,235 tons. *QM2*'s four electric propulsion pods (the biggest such installation to date, of course) have an output of 20 megawatts each for a design speed of 30 knots, a rough equivalent total of about 108,000 shp compared with *QM*'s 160,000 to drive her at 29 knots. In fact, of course, both vessels could exceed their design speed. Power for the pods comes from generators driven by four diesel engines which are used for cruising at moderate speeds, backed up by two gas turbines for higher speeds.

For lovers of trivial pursuits, 250 tonnes of paint went into the ship, along with 2,500 km of electrical cables, nearly 62 acres of carpet and 8,350 automatic fire extinguishers. After the old style of liner advertising, we are informed that her length is three times the height of St Paul's Cathedral and that her engine rooms generate enough electricity to supply the city of Southampton. Perhaps more important is the attention and expenditure which has been directed to the achievement of near-zero discharge of pollutants, whether from machinery, waste water or waste food The passenger capacity is 2,630 and the number of crew 1,253.

QM2 is not intended to replace the ageing but much-loved *QE2* , which remains in service in her cruising role.

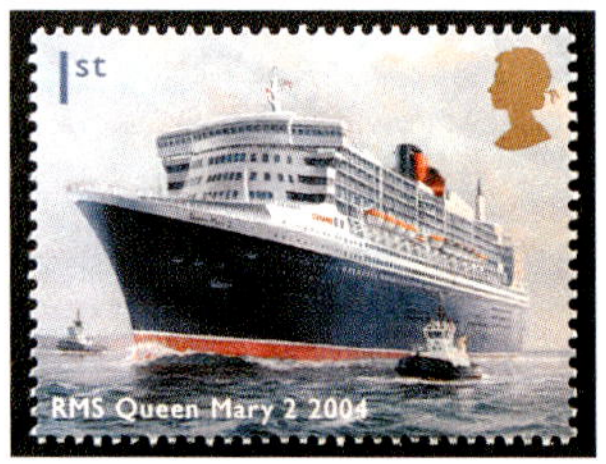

Ted was commissioned by The Royal Mail to produce the painting opposite, for use on this commemorative First Class postage stamp.

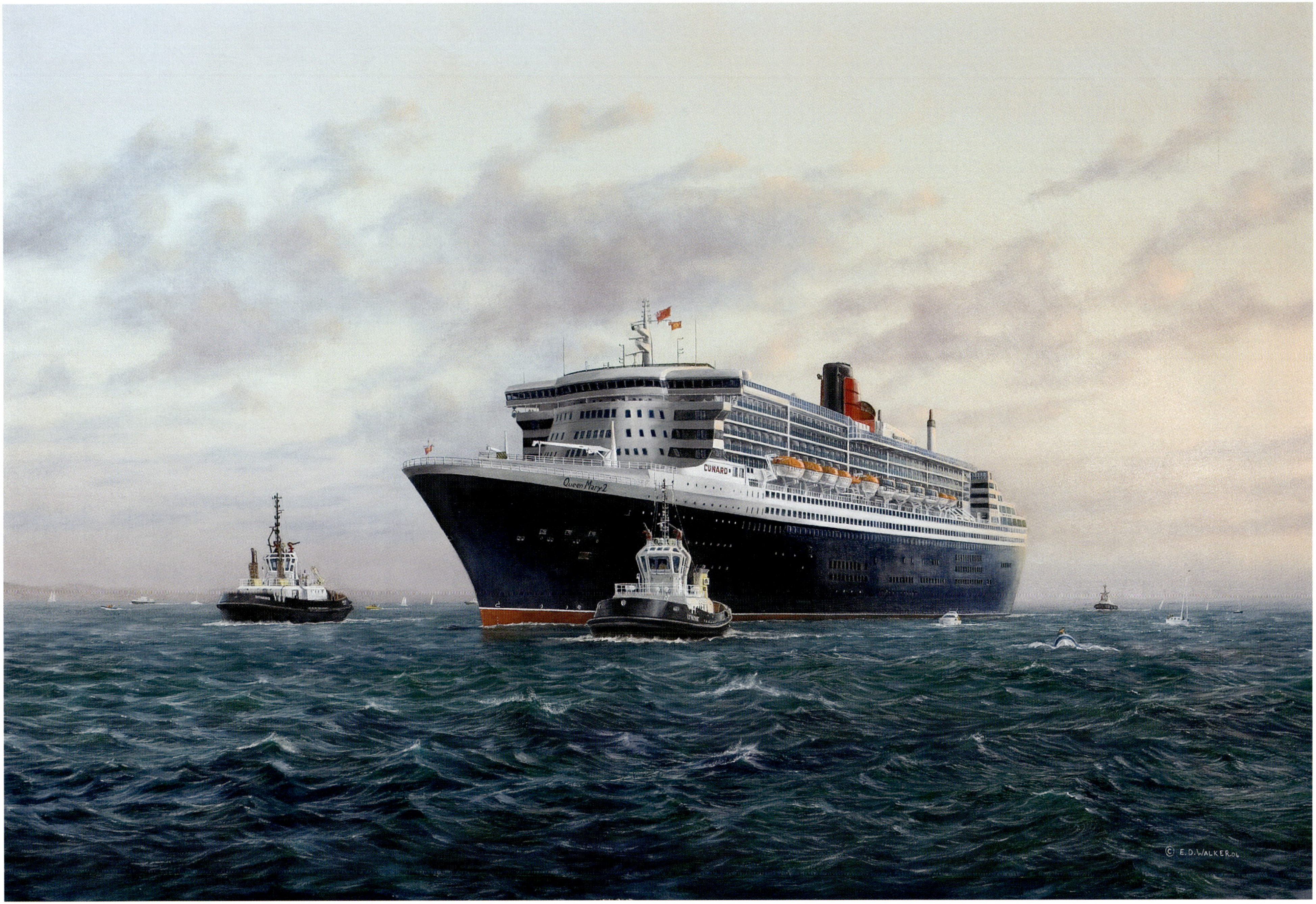
Queen Mary 2
CUNARD
© E.D.WALKER.06

Peleus leaving the Mersey

The 'Blue Funnel Line' was a classic case of an enterprise where all the cards of good fortune were in the founders' hands. The final end of the East India Company meant that the trade of south and east Asia beckoned enticingly, and the business, networking and engineering skills exhibited by Alfred and Philip Holt ensured that the invitation to open up those trades did not go begging. Just one of maritime history's great ironies is that it was the French who exhibited huge enthusiasm for constructing the Suez Canal and it was the British, led by the Holts, who made trading fortunes from it.

By the opening of last century, 'Blue Funnel' was among the largest shipping concerns in the world, still working in its slightly quaint way, basically as a family concern which prided itself on the superior qualities of its ships, its seagoing and shore-based staff – and its own way of doing things.

The end of the Second World War saw the company with a severely depleted fleet, needing to build or purchase about 22 good modern vessels, and the problem was exacerbated by the fact that those vessels which had served throughout the war were, of course, six years nearer to 'pensionable age'. *Peleus* was the leader of a class of four new vessels placed in service in 1949-50 which were intended to place Blue Funnel back in the lead in the Far East trade. *Peleus* and *Pyrrus* were built at Cammell Laird's. They mark a reversion to steam turbines in the interests of speed, which was wanted not just to attract custom, but to enable the four vessels to maintain a monthly service. At 18 knots they were the line's fastest vessels to date and could make the voyage from their last loading call at Rotterdam to Singapore in 20 days – five days better than P&O. This was also attractive to passengers, and they were fitted to carry 35 First Class (only). By the end of 1950, the combination of these ships with other classes enabled the traditional weekly service.

Blue Funnel continued to modernise their fleet, and also their shore facilities, notably at Vittoria Dock in Birkenhead. Unfortunately, while foreseeing the 'container revolution' they underestimated both its speed and its extent and were forced to give up traditional breakbulk carrying and seek the shelter of a container-based consortium, Ocean Container Lines. The four P-class vessels all went for scrap in 1972. It could be almost taken as a symbolic date marking the end of traditional cargoliner shipping as we knew it.

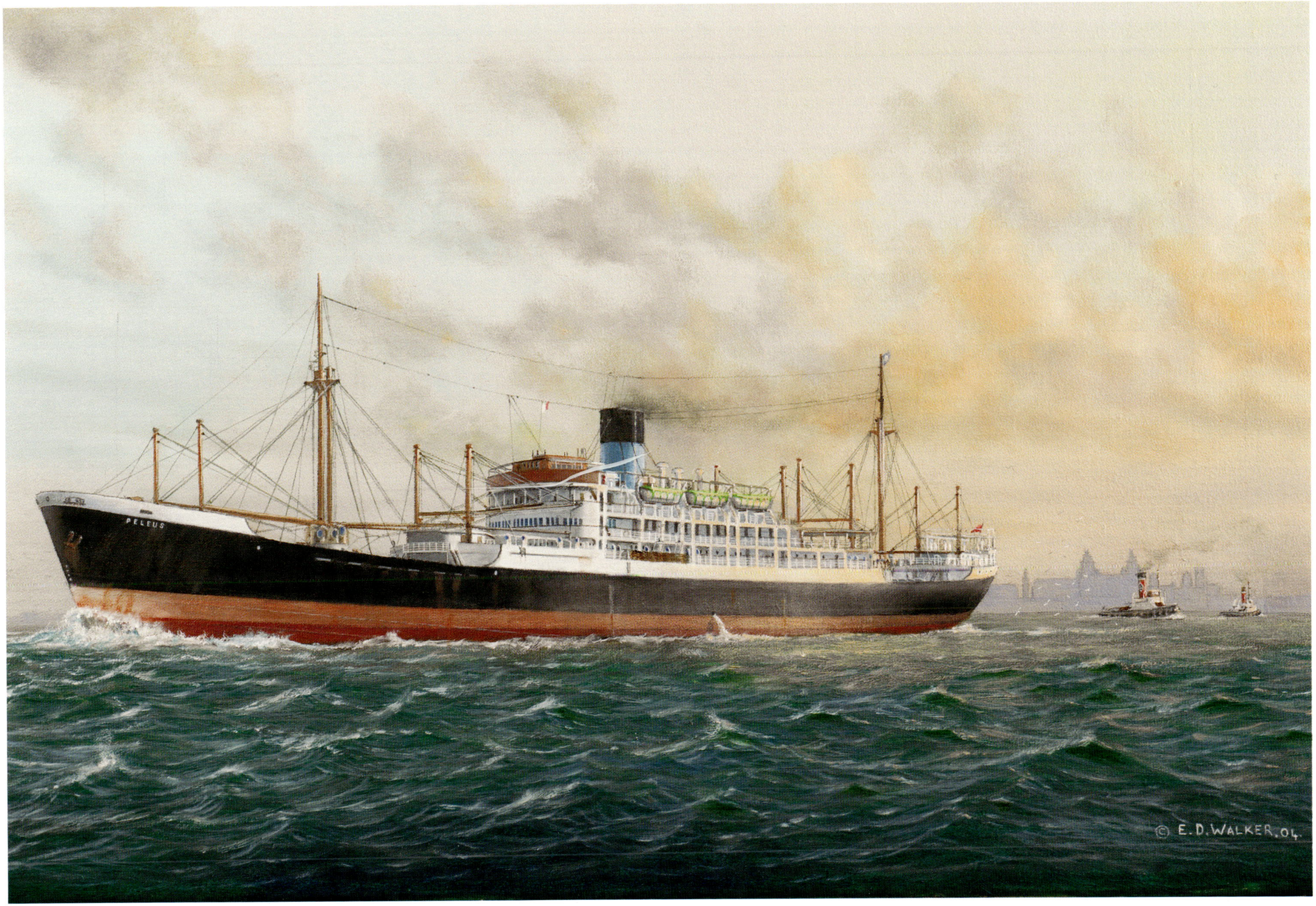
PELEUS
© E.D.WALKER.04.

Old Preston Docks

In the early days of port development, location was often determined by the lowest bridging point of a river, and so it was with Preston, lying some eight miles up the Ribble from the open sea. Although the river looks eminently navigable on a modern map, it was not so at the end of the eighteenth century, when the channel meandered about amid sandbanks and fairly frequently changed its meanders as well.

The first attempt to turn Preston into a 'modern' port was the establishment of the Ribble Navigation Company, which was to undertake embanking to fix the channel, but it was unsuccessful both physically and financially, and an ad hoc collaboration between the Corporation and some leading merchants brought about the building of the New Quays.

A second Ribble Navigation Company, established in 1838, commissioned a report from Robert Stevenson, the eminent Edinburgh lighthouse engineer. This seemed promising, but any idea of improvement was severely hit by the financial crash of 1847-48, eventually resulting in a third Company, which had an ambitious plan drawn up by Sir John Coode but could not raise the money to implement it. In 1883, the Corporation bought the Company out, and at last Preston became a serious international port, with a fully impounded and well-equipped dock of 30 acres, a small basin, a graving dock and a large timber pond. The latter was important as Preston gained the lion's share of the woodpulp trade of the north of England.

Woodburn, shown in the painting, was a three-masted steel barque of 1,552 gross tons. Built in 1896, she was 204 feet long and drew about 21 feet, which was moderately large for a sailing ship. She was owned by R. Shankland & Co of Port Glasgow, who had a fleet of eleven ships at the time, all sailing vessels and all with names ending in '...burn'. She was by no means their largest ship, and could be taken as fairly typical of sail's last hurrah in mainstream ocean trading. Yet she needs two tugs to get to sea, indicating that despite all the embanking work which had gone into the river, its navigation was still not a simple matter. That is one of the reasons why the Port of Preston was a drain on the town's rates from 1883 until 1955.

From then until the late '60s, trade was buoyant, assisted as in some other small-to-medium ports, by the severe labour problems which dogged the major ports. Ambitious plans were hatched (in the characteristically grandiose Dock Offices) to keep abreast of the 'shipping revolution', including the installation of a container crane, but, like the Port of Manchester, Preston failed to anticipate the speed and extent of the forthcoming changes. Trade dwindled during the '70s, sinking to almost nothing by 1980 and in 1981 the entire system was closed. It has since been re-developed in the usual 'mixed' manner, with housing, offices, a marina etc., so comprehensively that almost nothing recognisable remains of the port to which the crew of *Woodburn* would have looked back as they put to sea.

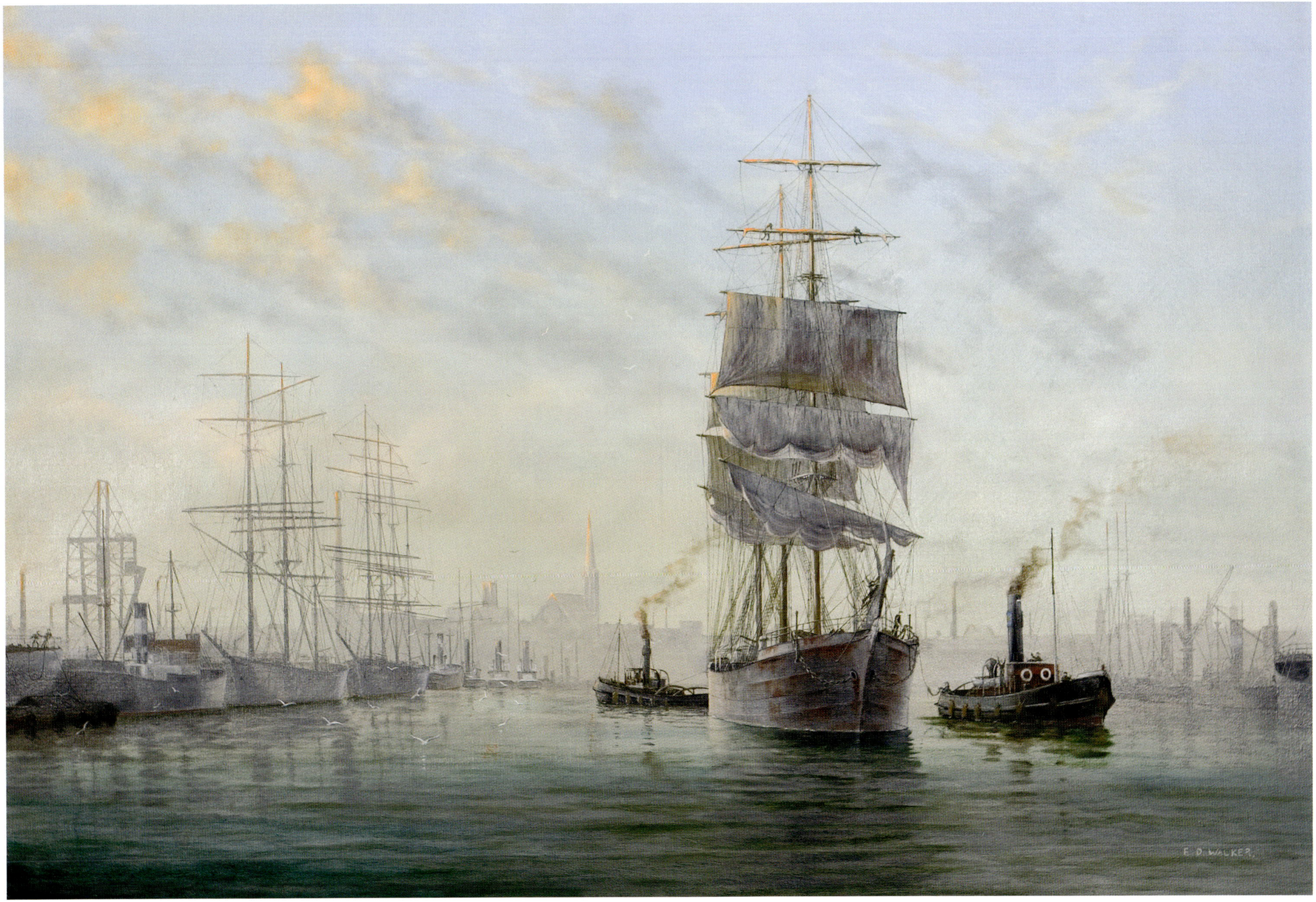
E. D. WALKER

The stranding of the *Mexico*

Mexico was a smallish 3-masted iron barque, 150ft long by 27.5ft wide, measuring 484 gross tons. She was built by T. R. Oswald of Sunderland in 1860 for Temperley's of London and was originally named *John Bull*. In 1880 she was sold to Ellis & Sons, also of London, who re-sold her in 1882 to Oetling Gebruder of Hamburg, who re-named her *Mexico*.

On 9 September 1886 she left Liverpool bound for South America and immediately after leaving the relative safety of the Mersey for the open waters of Liverpool Bay, she encountered extremely strong adverse winds and very poor visibility. Close to Southport she was driven onto a lee shore and so bad was the visibility, with mist, snow and hailstones, that she was actually aground before the captain had realised what was happening. It was reported that when the hail cleared a little he 'could see land on all sides'. The sea broke over the ship, smashing its bulwarks, and it seemed likely that she might break up. The Captain therefore fired distress rockets and dropped anchor in the hope that at least matters might get no worse. There was not much more he could do.

People often assume that shipwrecks mainly happen at sea, and of course many do, including most of the major 'lost with all hands' tragedies. However, if we look at numbers of accidents rather than number of deaths, a very different picture emerges. 'Safe home in port' is not just a cliché, but a downright lie, for most accidents to shipping happened in port, in the early stages of leaving it or the late stages of entering it. In 1881, for example, there were 62 'casualties', as the Liverpool Water Bailiff Returns styled them, and while some of these were trivial groundings or collisions, 16 were total losses. Unfortunately, no Returns were published for the year of *Mexico*'s stranding, but 1885 was the best year of the decade 1879-1888, with only 41 casualties and 13 total losses. But these figures do not tell the whole story: the Water Bailiff only recorded fatal accidents or those which endangered navigation, notably by stranding on the banks of the main channels in and out. In the 1890s, the percentage of accidents to British ships, worldwide, which happened in port varied between 6% and 11%. *Mexico* would be roughly as long at sea as she was safely tied up at each end of her voyage: we might assume a couple of weeks each while her time at risk while entering and leaving port was compressed into about a day in all. That day equalled the risks of virtually a whole month's voyaging and trading.

At first hearing it seems surprising, but it is not really. Collisions are far more likely when ships converge into port on the flow tide or when they are hurrying to make a late exit on the ebb. A skipper was more likely to take a risk putting to sea in unfavourable weather if he had been sitting in dock or anchored in the river awaiting a favourable wind, losing money every moment he sat anchored there. In the river, there was the additional, now-extinct, risk of a 'pea-souper', a 'smog' so thick that it was hard to see well enough to walk safely, never mind move ships around.

It is also a mistake to think that Liverpool Bay is the sheltered place it might appear on a map. Just five years after *Mexico* stranded, the 3-masted ship *Hannah Landles* sailed from Liverpool, under tow, and encountered the worst Liverpool Bay could throw at her: she gradually drifted towards the Great Burbo Bank, and letting go the anchors made no difference because the force of the sea snapped the cables. She was swept over the bank and then dropped onto it from a considerable height by seas which were mountainous by inshore standards: she stuck, and the huge seas broke clean over her. Outstanding skill and courage on the part of the crew of the tug and of the Liverpool and New Brighton lifeboats enabled the rescue of all the crew.

Continued on Page 48.

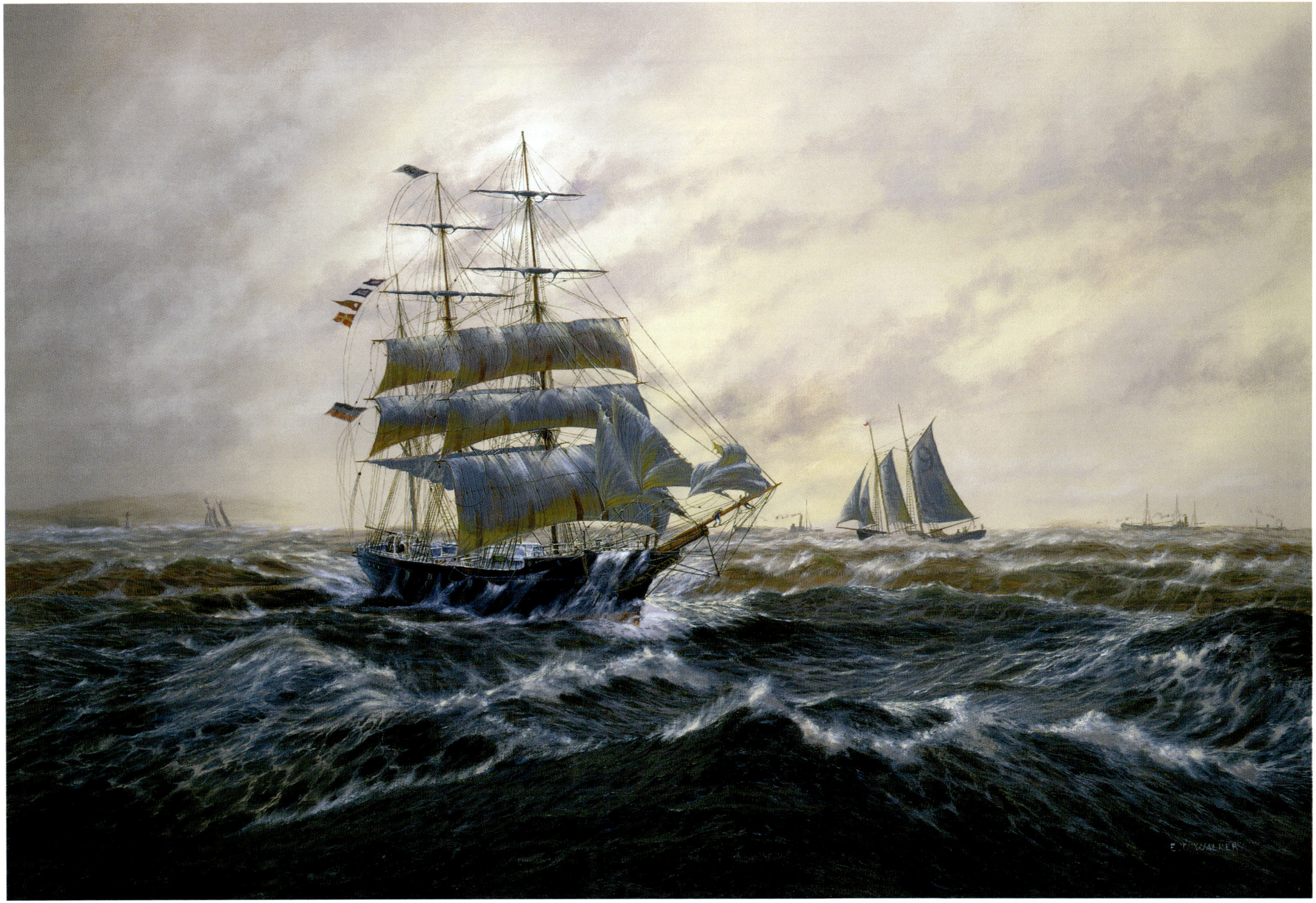

The stretch of coast where *Mexico* stranded was a notorious trap for the unwary or the unfamiliar and it was exceedingly difficult, once a ship had stranded there, to get it off again. So far, it sounds like a pretty routine accident, in an age when seafarers had to accept that 'these things happen'.

But this was to become a very special maritime tragedy. In response to the distress rockets, three lifeboats were launched, from Southport, Lytham and St. Anne's. The Lytham boat succeeded in rescuing the crew of the *Mexico*, but both the *Eliza Fearnley* of Southport and the *Laura Janet* of St Anne's were capsized and the boats, working to the lee side of the Mexico and in fairly shallow water, did not have space to right themselves. Thirteen of the sixteen men on the Southport boat were drowned as were all fourteen of those on the St Anne's boat. It was one of the blackest nights in the history of the lifeboat service, and probably unique in combining 27 deaths with the rescue of all the crew of the original casualty. The proceedings of the inquest produced the usual sad spectacle: because lifeboatmen are usually tight little communities, a high proportion of the victims were relatives of other victims, so that women had, for example, to go and identify the bodies of their husband and their son. Even in the words of the hard-baked hacks of a trade paper like *Lloyds List* the localisation of tragedy is clear.

The *Mexico* did not break up where she stranded: contrary to what one might have expected, in March 1887 she was raised, towed to Preston and sold to William Allsop & Sons for £45, who repaired and re-fitted her and sold her to J. Morrow of Glasgow in 1890. She was sold three times more: her last owner re-named her *Valhalla*, which was rather tempting fate. On 27 February 1900 she was wrecked at Tantallon on the Firth of Fourth, Scotland, and this time it was permanent.

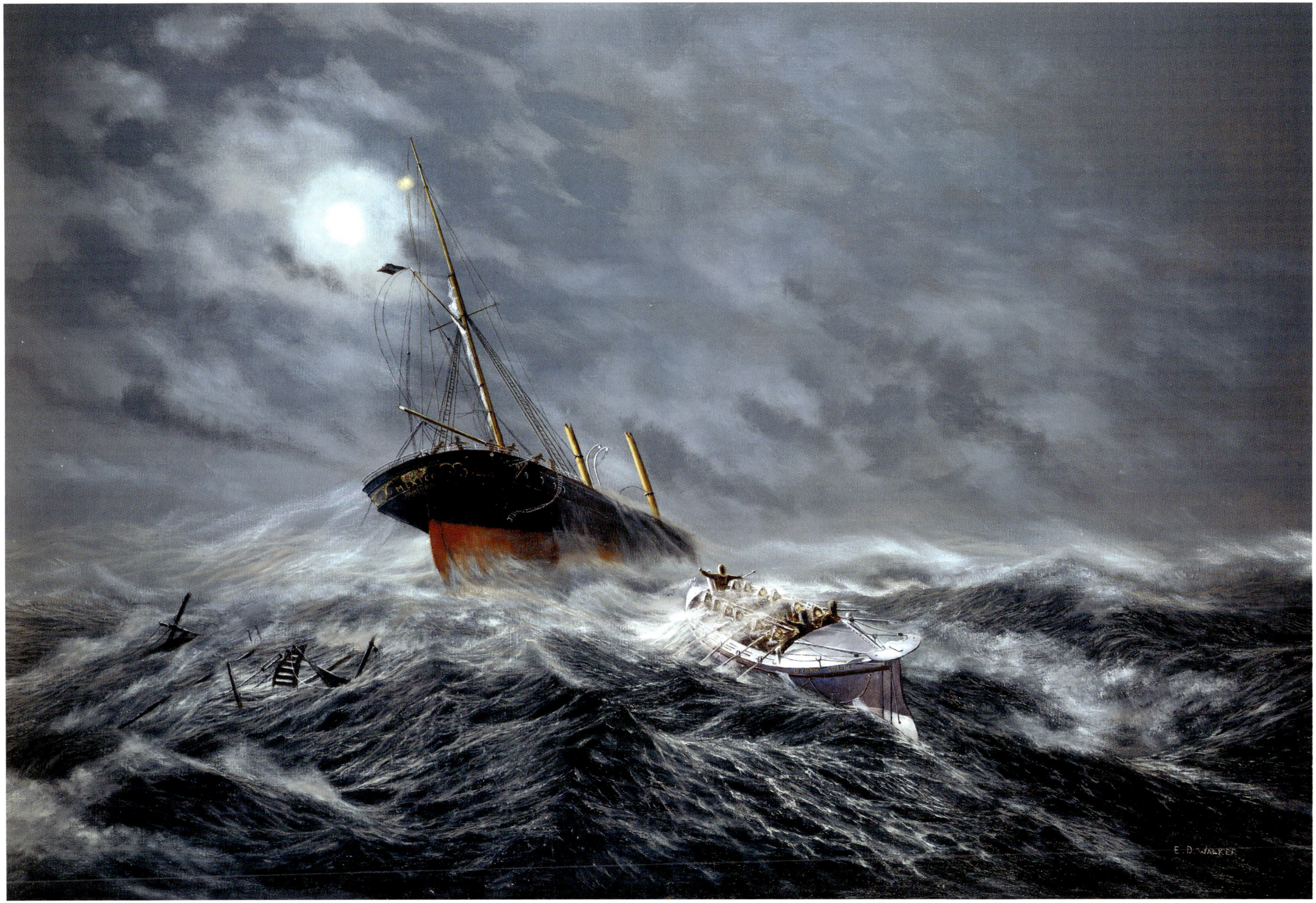
E.D. WALKER

Liverpool off Point Linas, picking up the pilot

This is a broadly similar view to that shown on page 17, but a decade or so earlier, before sail entered its terminal decline. The pilot schooner is standing off to port of *Liverpool* and the boarding punt may be seen in transit between.

Liverpool was built in 1889 by Russell & Co. of Port Glasgow. She was a four-masted full-rigged ship of 3,400 gross tons, 333 ft long, 47.9 ft wide and with a draught of 26.5 ft. These dimensions placed her among the largest sailing ships ever built. She was originally owned by the Sailing Ship Liverpool Company Ltd., but managed by R. W. Leyland & Co. This was quite a common device at the time: it meant that if the *Liverpool* were lost at sea with some hugely valuable cargo, only the 'single ship company' and not the whole of the 'Leyland Line', would go down with it. In the year before *Liverpool* went into service, Leyland's managed 21 sailing ships.

Ralph Leyland was an interesting man and possessed a singular entrepreneurial skill. Shipowning and trading was an intensely cyclical business, and if trade fell, so did first freight rates and then the value of ships. The knack was to succeed in what is nowadays known as counter-cyclical spending by investing in new ships when prices were low, such that they would be completed when the market had risen. Leyland had that knack, and it made him a major figure – for a time. He was also very much aware of the move to steam, but continued to invest in very large sailing ships: there had been discussion of building *Liverpool* as a five-masted ship, a rig which was adopted on only one giant vessel, the *Preussen*. Quite soon, his instincts told him it was time to change, and *Riversdale*, a steel three-masted ship built in 1893, was his last new sailing vessel, and the following year his first steamer, *Planet Mercury*, went into service.

Unfortunately, Ralph Leyland was not a one-man band, and in 1896 the single-ship companies were all consolidated into the Leyland Company, which, in effect, was a sale of his share to pay debts incurred as a result of his brother's activities. The result was the familiar process of 'corporatisation', with the running of the business passing from the hands of sharp-end entrepreneurs to those of salaried managers. This did not, however, stop the 'Leyland Line' being the largest payer of Liverpool port dues in the Edwardian years.

Liverpool was built primarily for the jute trade and could carry about 26,000 bales. Her maiden voyage was to Melbourne, where she loaded wool, wheat, flour and other goods for Calcutta, where she loaded jute jor Dundee, whence she went to Frederickstadt and loaded timber for Melbourne.

On 25 February 1902 she was wrecked off Alderney while on passage from Antwerp to San Francisco. She had grounded quite gently and seemed eminently salvageable, but began to break up and soon became a total loss.

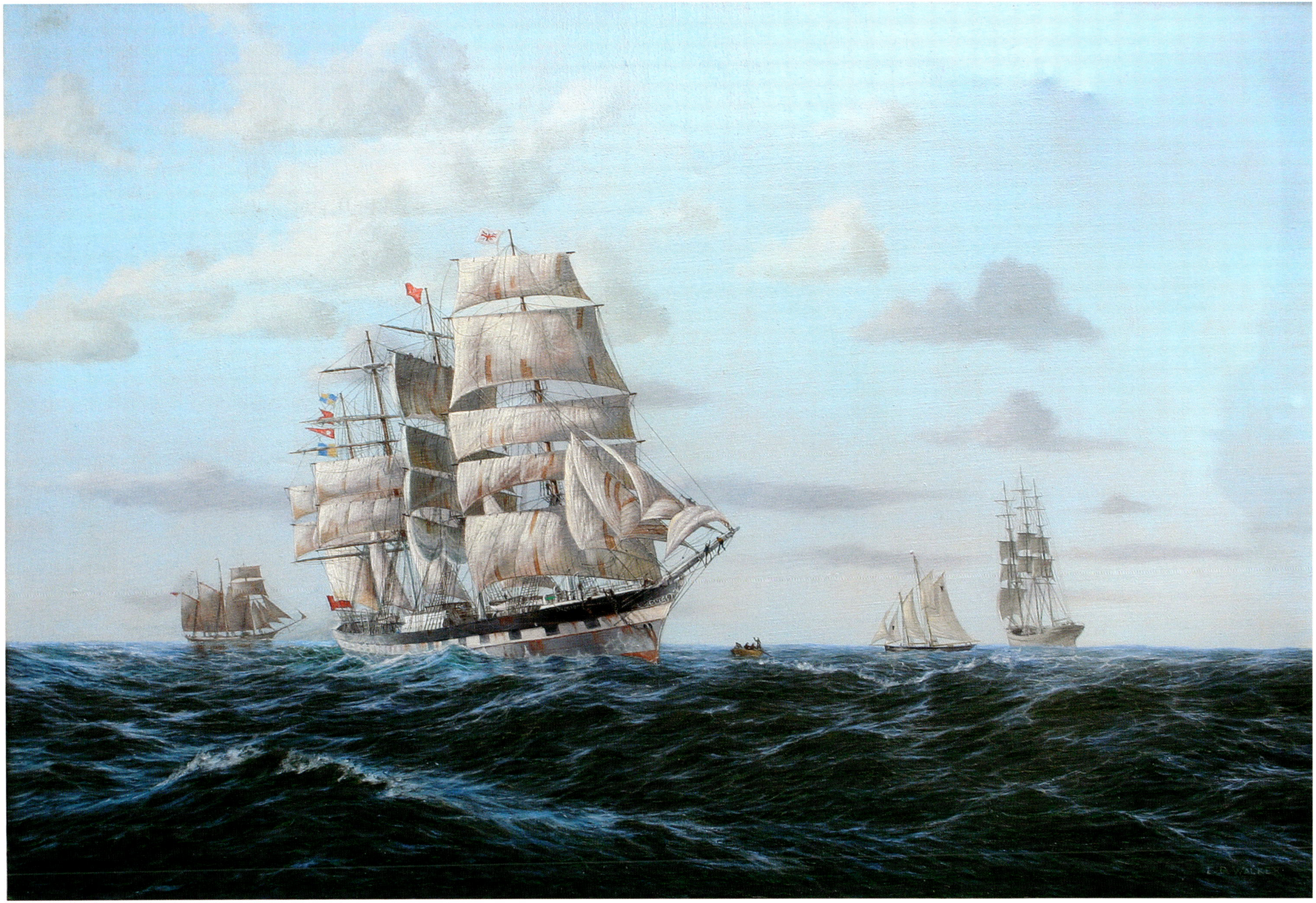

Royal Charter

Royal Charter was a large, fast ship of the sort that people argue about: can you call it a 'clipper' or can you not? She was a 3-masted full-rigged ship, built of iron in 1855 at Sandycroft on the River Dee for the well-known Liverpool Australia traders, Gibbs, Bright & Co. She was 336 feet long, with a length:beam ratio of 7 and a very sleek hull-line. Because her intended voyage was Liverpool–Australia, she was equipped with a 200 hp auxiliary steam engine with a lifting screw, which could be used to maintain progress when the wind was insufficient while saving fuel when it was not.

Her early history was unhappy, but she began her maiden voyage to Australia on 26 January 1856, and soon proved not only a sound ship but a very fast one: at one stage she averaged very nearly 15 knots for 30 hours together. She eventually arrived in Melbourne in minimally under 60 days, at a time when 90 days was a very good passage. The reason for the interest in Melbourne was, of course, the Gold Rush, so when *Royal Charter* set out for Liverpool on 26 August 1859 she was carrying a lot of people with business back home and others who had already made enough to retire on. There was also a considerable amount of gold: about £322,000 in the strong room and a lot more in passengers' personal effects.

The ship reached Queenstown in 58 days – soon enough to make another 60-day passage to Liverpool – and when she left there were 112 crew and about 380 passengers aboard for the last short leg. She had been facing severe weather as she approached Holyhead, but this was a ship which could race along in the notorious storms of the Southern Ocean and had rounded Cape Horn on her present trip. What hit her next was quite exceptional: the wind not only rose to full hurricane force, but suddenly changed direction such that *Royal Charter* had nowhere to run from it: Captain Taylor attempted to anchor and use his engine to keep his stem to the wind – this is the phase of the approaching disaster shown in the painting - but the force of the wind and the waves it was whipping up was irresistible and the ship was driven aground.

Just ten yards of seething surging water lay between the ship and the shore, and with the help of men from the village of Moelfre, a Maltese seaman named Joseph Rodgers got a line ashore, allowing a bosun's chair to be rigged. But the conditions were so rough that only 16 of about 360 passengers survived, together with 18 crew and five out of 11 riggers who were working their passage home. Very few of the dead were drowned: nearly all were either crushed when the ship began to break up or battered to death on the rocks when the sea swept them from the ship, the bosun's chair or the rocks themselves. *Royal Charter* was only the worst loss among many that night: around the coasts of Britain, 132 other ships were sunk and the total loss of life was about 800.

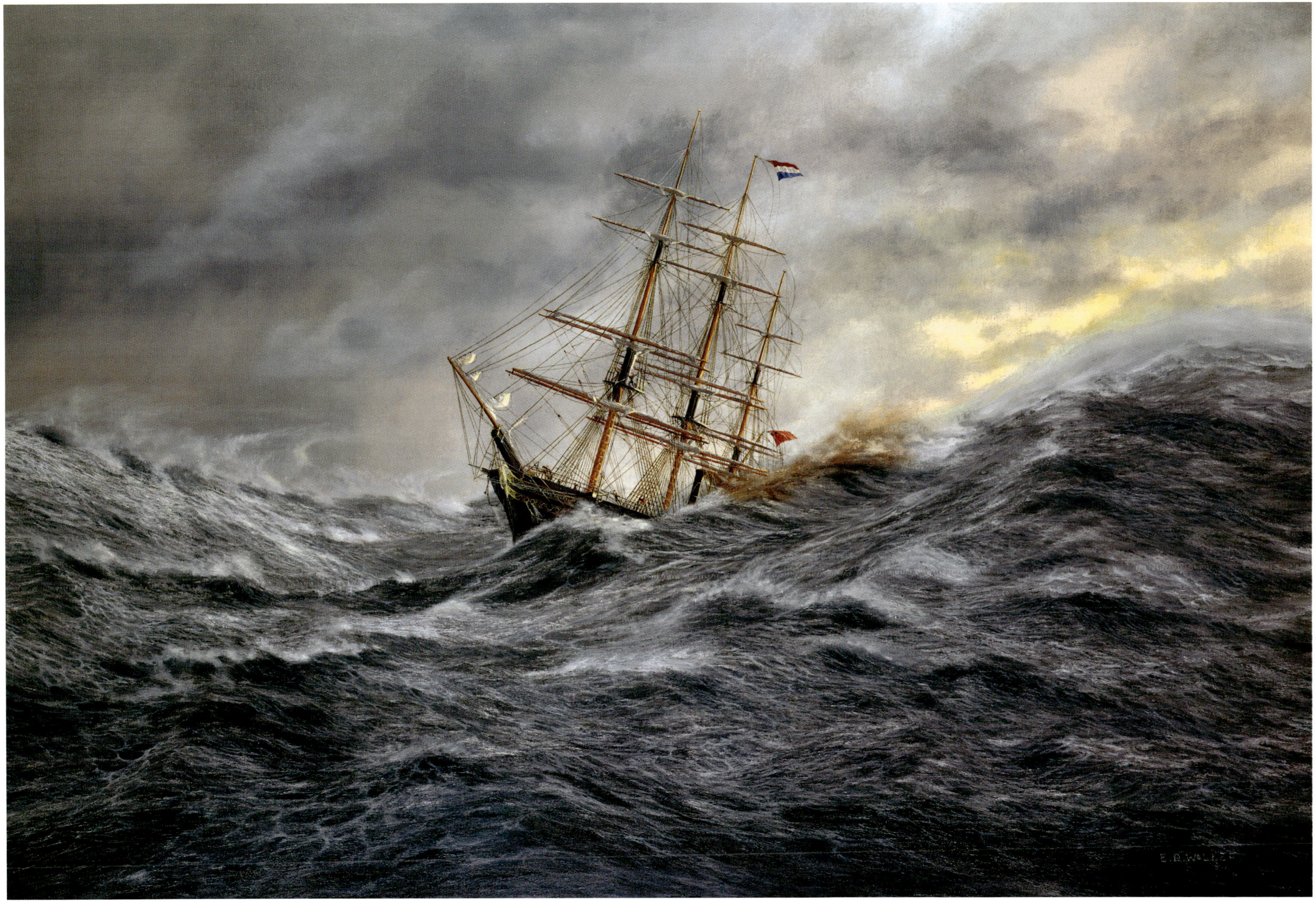

Moshulu: the last grain race

The 'racing' of long-haul sailing cargo vessels grew up as a question of being first to market with the new growth of a seasonal cargo, among which the tea clippers are much the best known. By 1900, the grain trade had become largely de-seasonalised, with a futures market in existence and cargoes often being 'sold at sea'. Speed was not of the essence, and if it had been then steamships would have been used. Why race?

Moshulu was launched by William Hamilton & Co., at Port Glasgow on 18 April 1904. She was a large (3,116 gross tons) steel 4-masted barque for F. H. J. Siemens of Hamburg and was originally named *Kurt*. She was cleverly designed and equipped to operate with minimum crew numbers: she stood 198 ft tall in drydock – 'from keel to truck' and had 31 sails with a total area about 45,000 square ft. yet could still sail half way round the world with a crew of Captain, three mates, one sailmaker/bosun, two donkeymen (who had charge of the mechanical equipment), carpenter, Steward, Steward's boy, 18 foremast hands, five boys and four apprentices. From these 37, two watches had to be formed to steer the vessel - and attend to 39 items of running rigging.

While not possessed of extreme clipper lines or go-faster devices like studding-sails or skysails, she was not a slow ship and could log 15 knots.

After the Great War there were fewer and fewer places for old sailing ships to go, and in 1935, *Moshulu*, along with other famous old ships, ended up being owned in that time-warp of ocean sail which was Mariehamn, Aland Islands. Unlike most of her contemporaries, her best performance, and the voyage which would earn her undying fame, was yet to come.

On 18 October 1938 she sailed from Belfast in ballast and arrived in Port Lincoln on 8 January. Like some of her competitors, including *Pamir* and *Passat*, she took a while finding a cargo, not sailing (from Port Victoria) until 11 March. She arrived in Queenstown on 10 June, a passage of 91 days. By way of comparison, the famous *Archibald Russell* took 121 days. *Moshulu's* was not the fastest passage ever, (that was by *Padua* in the incredible time of 66 days in 1933) but she won by a margin of two days in what would turn out to be the last grain race.

So why did they race? Nearly all the 'contestants' belonged to Gustav Erikson, so it was hardly likely to be a contest for business. But the shipowner or captain who was still in sail in the 1930s was scarcely going to be there solely for the money: they were there in part for the pride of operating one of man's greatest inventions, the sailing ship, to the limits of its, and their, capability.

There was another dimension to it: racing attracted the attention of nostalgic young gentlemen who wanted to go to sea under sail while they still could, to which end they would sign on as apprentices, who paid a premium (commonly of £50) and received a derisory wage of around ten shillings (50 pence) a month. On *Moshulu's* record voyage there were four such aboard, only one of them a Finn.

The painting shows *Moshulu* with all sails set: in the background is her rival *Passat*, formerly owned by the famous Hamburg firm of Laeisz, bought by Erikson in 1932.

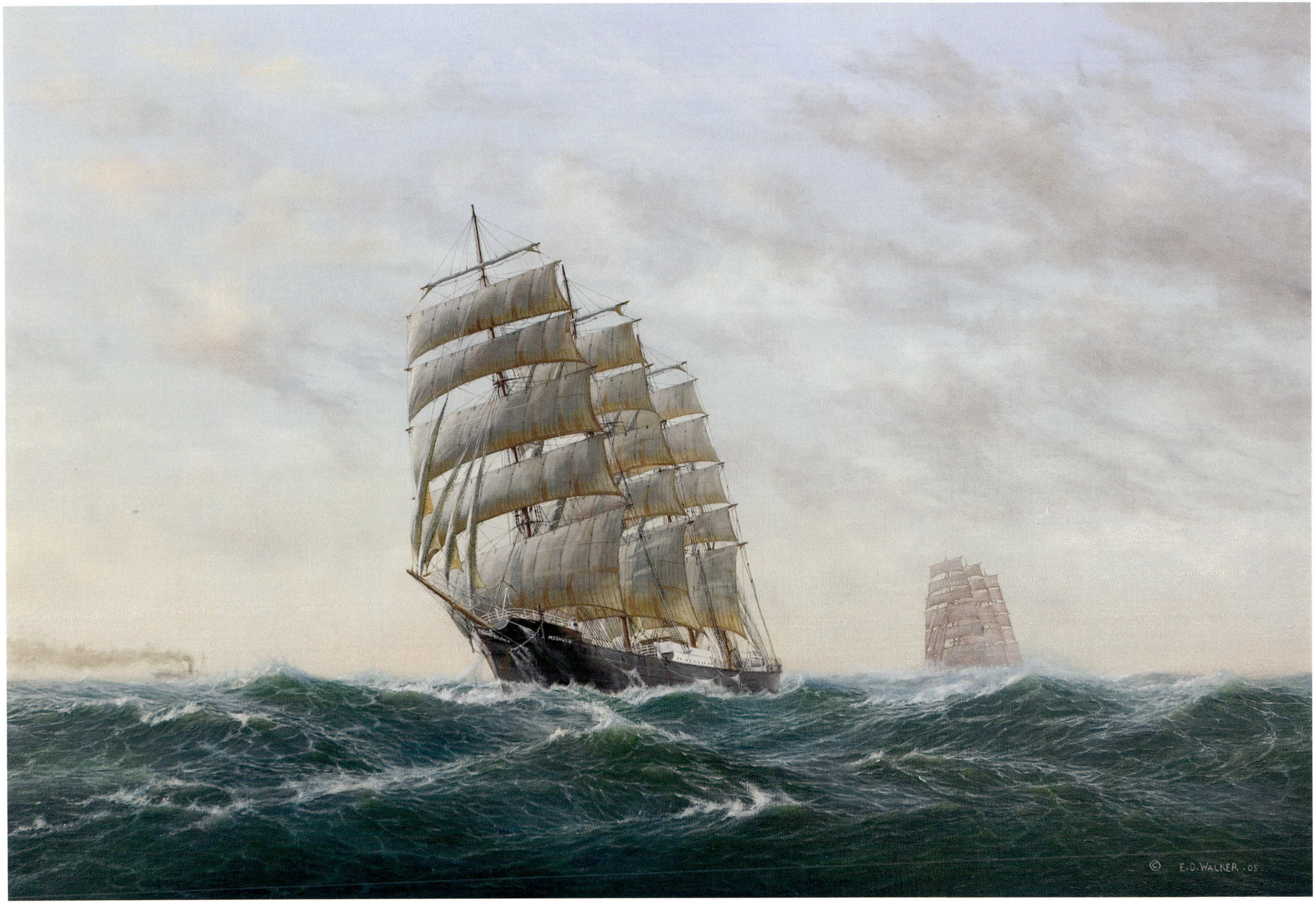
© E.D.WALKER .05

Gran Regata Columbus

The Cutty Sark Tall Ships race was already the longest-running and most famous event of its kind when preparations were first put in hand to celebrate the five hundredth anniversary of Columbus' landing in the New World. It was becoming almost historic in its own right, for having the same sponsor for thirty years, as it did, was a record for any sporting event. It is organised by Sail Training International, which sounds easy if you say it quickly, but organising between 70 and 100 vessels with a total of about 4,000 crew coming from over 30 nations is no simple matter. It was a natural move to combine the two events, and the route agreed upon involved two starting points, Genoa and Lisbon, with the entrants from both uniting at Cadiz, whence they sailed to Las Palmas, St Juan, New York and Liverpool.

The painting shows a group of the largest tall ships in the world. The large vessel in the foreground is the Polish full-rigged ship *Dar Mlodziezy*, built of steel at Gdansk in 1982 and owned by the Merchant Marine Academy there. She measures 2,385 gross tons and is 86.7 metres long by 14.01 metres wide. Specifically constructed for the training of merchant navy officers, she is designed to cruise at 11 knots, with a maximum of 12.5 knots, and is equipped with a fairly powerful auxiliary motor (1,500 bhp Sulzer diesel) to enable her to keep to schedule in the event of insufficient wind. She is among the most-travelled of tall ships, including a round-the-world trip in 1987-88 in celebration of the bicentenary of the foundation of Australia. The nearest vessel in the background is the Portuguese *Sagres II*, while that to the right is *Sedov*, one of the big Russian four-masted barques, of broadly similar design to *Kruzenshtern*, the large black and white vessel in the left distance.

Sagres II, originally named *Albert Leo Schlageter*, is a 3-masted barque, built of steel by Blohm & Voss at Hamburg, as a sail training vessel for the German Navy. She is 266.75ft long and displaces 1,865 tons. After World War II she served with the Brazilian Navy and was acquired in 1962 by the Portuguese Navy, which still owns and operates her.

Unlike the majority of sail training vessels, which are purpose-built, *Sedov* began life as a cargo vessel, built by Germania Werft of Kiel for F. A. Vinnen of Bremen in 1921, and named *Magdalene Vinnen*, later changed to *Kommodore Johnsen*. She is, by sailing ship standards, huge: 328.8 ft long by 48ft wide and with a gross tonnage of 3,476. Built of steel, she is rigged as a four-masted barque and was, unusually, equipped with an auxiliary diesel engine from the beginning. But effective as these big sailing ships were on long-haul voyages, the 1930s saw the end of most of them and severe difficulty for the rest. *Kommodore Johnsen* managed to continue following conversion into a dual-purpose vessel – sail training and cargo in 1930. She survived the war and was handed to the Soviet Union for use as a sail training vessel, which duty she still performs, albeit now for a different master.

The scene in the painting is of the formation of the 'Grand Parade of Sail' when the vessels were about to leave at the end of their stay in Liverpool.

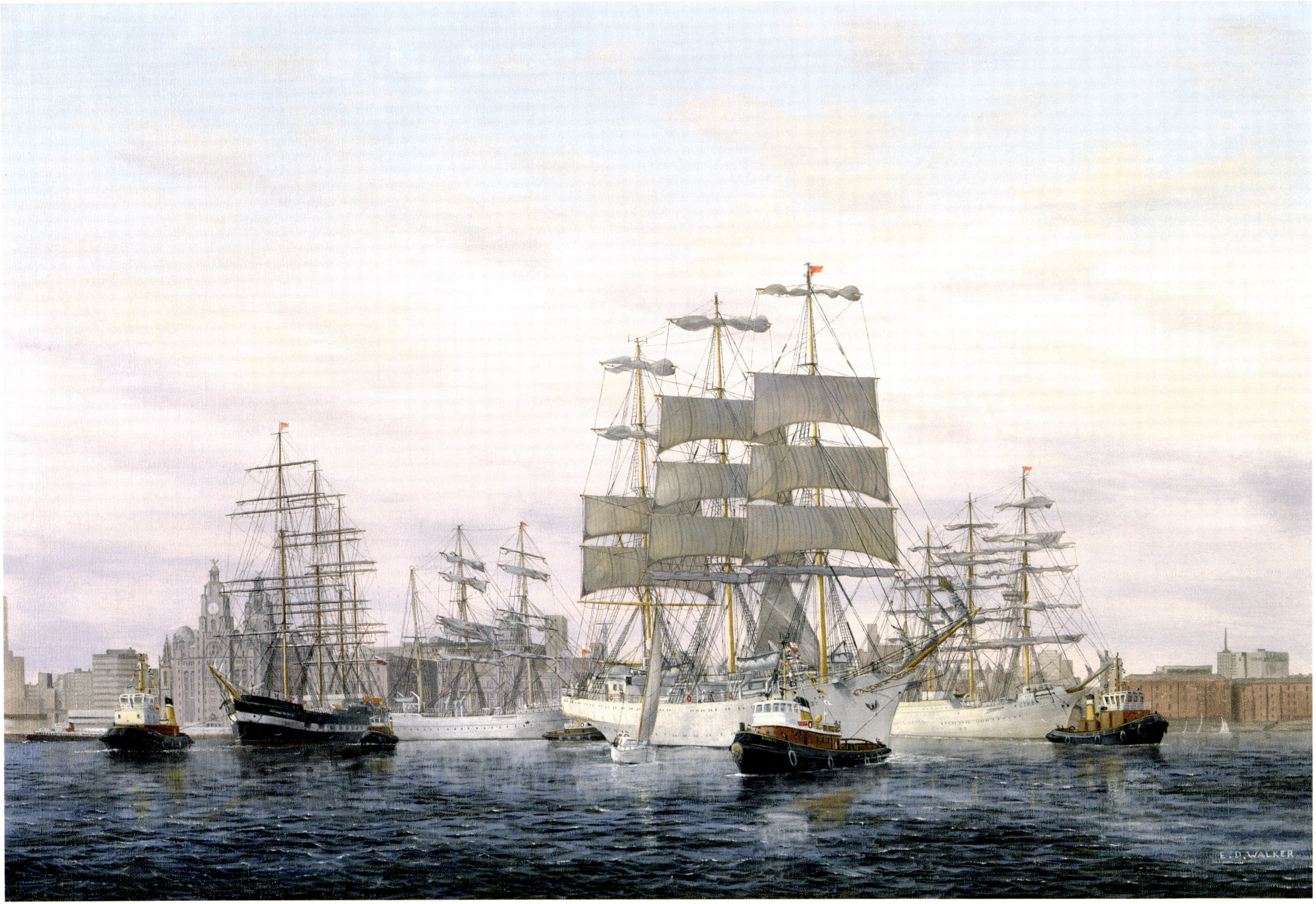
E. D. WALKER

Juan Sebastian de Elcano at the Pier Head

Juan Sebastian de Elcano was a purpose-built sail training vessel, launched in 1927 and commissioned into the Spanish Navy the following year. She is a four-masted topsail schooner, built of steel, and with a hull length of 289ft and a displacement tonnage of 3,750 she is among the larger 'Tall Ships' afloat today. She came to Liverpool in 1992 as part of the 'Gran Regata Columbus', which celebrated the five hundredth anniversary of Christopher Columbus' landing in the New World.

One might query the purpose of building STVs for the Spanish (or any other) navy of the twentieth century, well advanced into the age of steel and steam. It was already clear by 1921 that the future of ocean-going sailing vessels was pretty much limited to Mariehamn and that even that 'future' was probably pretty short term. The purpose of teaching cadets, apprentices or future Kings the skills of reefing in a topsail is not immediately apparent, when the skills needed in future deck officers, apart from those common to any form of navigation or ship operation, included basic knowledge of the mysteries of the Chief Engineer's domain, including such non-romantic things as electric or hydraulic deck winches. A sailing ship was not going to be an invaluable teaching aid for swinging out the lifeboats of a warship or a passenger liner. Was the reason sail training continued in so many parts of the world simply that the decision-makers in matters of training were old men who had trained in sail when sail was still for real, and thought that working a steam (or motor) vessel was rearing a generation of softies?

We have to disentangle two different reasons here. HMS *Conway*, the Mercantile Marine Service Association's famous officer cadet training vessel, formerly anchored in the Mersey, opened on 1 August 1859. There were very sound reasons for using an old warship (she was a sixth-rate frigate of 652 tons, built in 1832) as 'premises' for training aspiring merchant navy deck offices: she was a gift from the Admiralty and her masts, rigging and equipment were valuable teaching aids at a time when the majority of ships were still under sail. Demand twice outgrew the accommodation and the third and last HMS Conway, which was put into service in 1876, had been the full 'line of battle' ship, HMS *Nile*. Sail was still numerically predominant, but steam was growing fast. The period from then to the outbreak of the great war was one of extremely rapid technical change which often provided opportunities to buy obsolete steamers for cheap. Might this, perhaps, have been time for another change?

Despite the advantages of using an old ship, it was far from essential: the year *Conway* opened as a school ship, the shore-based Liverpool Sailors' Home Navigation School enrolled 664 boys, making it by far the largest of its kind in the country, and later, when the Liverpool Nautical College was opened by Liverpool Borough Council under the terms of the Technical Instruction Act of 1889, it, too was shore-based. If what was needed was to teach boys how to navigate, how to check up on the Bosun's black arts of cargo handling, how to ensure that the crew got enough food to keep them healthy but not a pennyworth more, could all be learned ashore? At the other end of the scale, however, sail training as we understand it today was already happening: Lord Brassey established an eponymous Ocean Training Scheme in 1890 which survived until 1914.

Continued on Page 60.

As a young man, King Juan Carlos of Spain, had trained on the Juan Sebastian de Elcano. The reproduction oppposite is from an original painting presented to the king on the occasion of the ship's visit to Liverpool in 1992. The famous 'Pier Head Trio' of the Dock Offices, Cunard Building and Royal Liver Building is prominent in the background, in the happy days before some clot thought of calling them the 'three graces'.

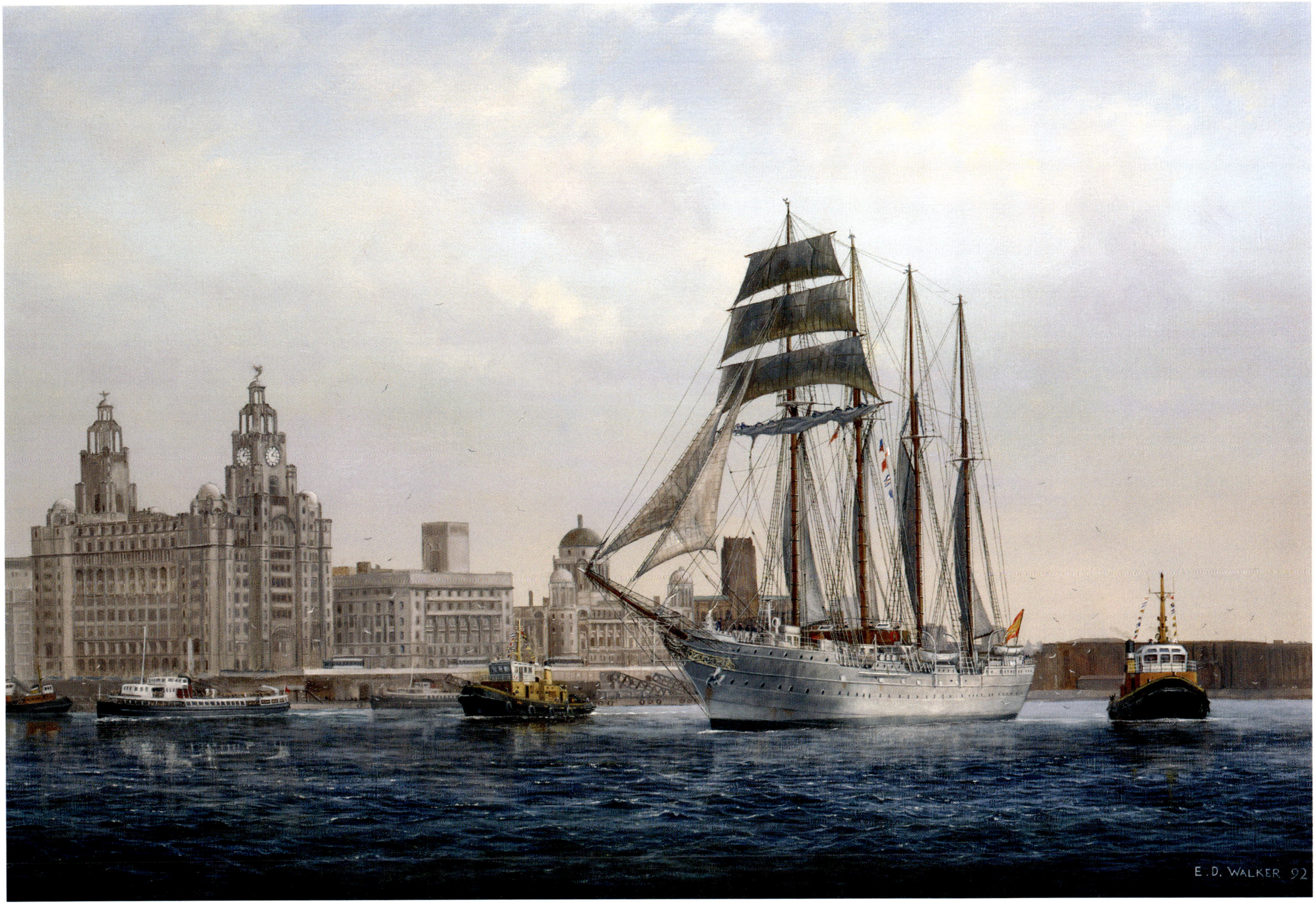
E.D. WALKER 92

Race Fever

Which brings us to the second reason for the apparently anomalous interest in sail, namely the suggestion that there are important things and attitudes which are learned better - some might say only - under sail than any other way. Handling a ship for maximum progress while maintaining safety can probably still only be learned at sea, increasingly sophisticated electronic simulators notwithstanding. It can, however, be learned aboard a modern motor vessel, up to a point. Consider an analogy: it used to be a common practice in mechanical engineering workshops to make apprentices learning to use an ordinary centre lathe do some of their work on a treadle lathe. There was a very sound reason for this: maximum stock removal is achieved by careful choice of tool form, cutting angle, and height of mounting, in conjunction with careful sharpening and correct speed.

Using a power lathe, minor errors are concealed by the lack of feedback from contact with the job: using a treadle lathe the apprentice could feel the difference between correct setting and 'that'll do' sloppiness in a direct and physical manner.

So it is with sail. The sailing ship was the biggest and most complex application of traditional craft skills in history, and it was the largest way of harvesting free power until the large hydro-electric stations of the 1920s. Down to the end of wooden shipbuilding, a period which included some of the legendary tea clippers, these wonderful structures continued to be built using only hand tools. But their working as well as their construction required the skilful blending of a number of variables. When the captain got it right - the right amount of sail set and the right course - he was getting maximum work out of the vessel with minimum strain on the rigging and the structure of the hull, to say nothing of the crew. He could feel this, just as the apprentice turner could feel when he had it right. It is not an obsolete skill: structural failure of ships in exceptionally bad weather conditions are happily rare now compared with those of the age of sail, but they do still happen, and a man who can read the wind and the sea better than another is likely to be a safer as well as a quicker captain.

The modern generation of STVs do not purport to provide that: Sail Training International was created in 1956 to organise the the first international race for sail training Tall Ships. Some of these vessels belonged to various navies, for reasons given above, but others did not, existing instead to provide sailing ship experience for people who had not the slightest intention of going to sea as a career. Seventeen nations have representatives on the board of Sail Training International, but that is far from the full extent of sail training, for Russia has no representative yet is home to three huge ships, two of which appear elsewhere in this book, namely *Kruzenshtern* and *Sedov* and there are further tall ships based in another dozen or so countries.

What the STVs offer to the 'amateur' crew members might be thought to be just a more capital-intensive version of nineteenth century 'muscular Christianity', a promise to 'turn boys into men'. It's a very physical business which can involve a lot of cold, wet and hardship, to say nothing of exhaustion. A bit like rugby, really. Except, that is, when you try to cheat, for unlike a rugby referee, Mother Nature is all-seeing and unforgiving. Get it really wrong and she brandishes the red card which sends you to the lifeboats. The crew ethos is and must be, one of heavy dependence on each other to do it right. That's what it has come to be about, and it works. If it works now, then it very probably worked for the Spanish Navy in 1927.

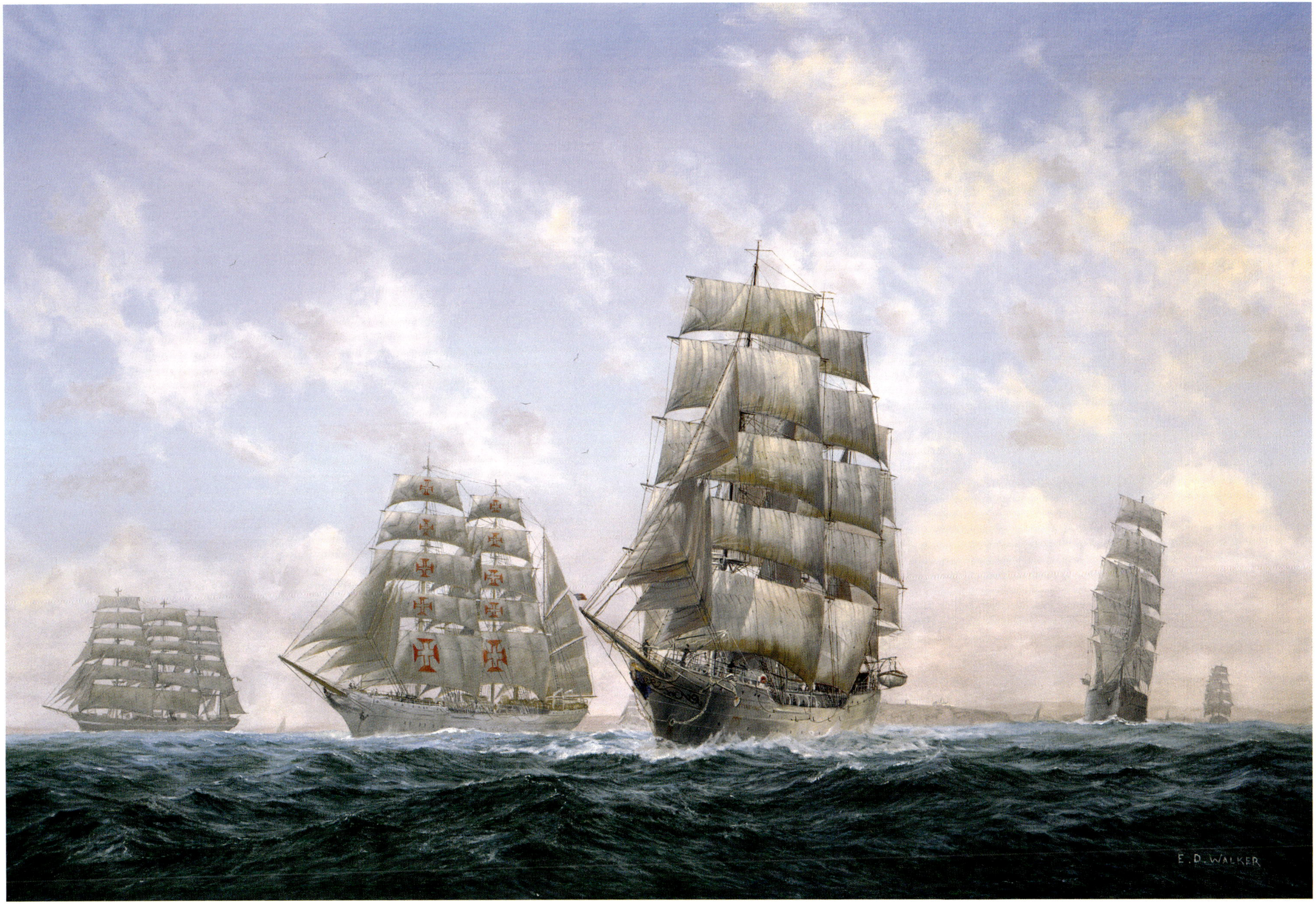
E.D. WALKER

CSS *Alabama* on sea trials in the Mersey

When the American Civil War broke out in 1861, President Lincoln almost immediately ordered a naval blockade of the Confederate ports, which the South's negligible navy was largely unable to challenge. Shrewdly, the Confederates adopted that traditional resort of the weaker power in a naval conflict, commerce raiding. This forced the superior power either to watch its merchant fleet being steadily eroded by the raiders, or to deploy quite disproportionately heavy resources in trying to hunt down and destroy the raiders. Because a blockade of the Confederate ports would seriously disrupt the supply of cotton, Liverpool was a fairly intelligent place for the Confederacy to send an agent, one James Dunwoody Bulloch, on a mission to purchase warships

They could be reasonably sure that Liverpool men would be sympathetic to the Confederacy, and they were. Bulloch ordered a total of six warships, of which by far the most notorious, because the most successful, was *Alabama*, a wooden screw steamer of 1,040 tons, built at Laird Brothers' yard in Birkenhead. The North knew about her, and did their best to prevent her delivery, but were not quite fast enough. On 29 July, *Alabama*, still known only by her Yard number, 290 or by the pseudonym *Enrica*, was taken out on sea trials, never to return. In Moelfre Bay, Anglesey, she put ashore various guests and put to sea.

At the Azores she took on board the coal, guns and stores which were necessary for the next stage of the operation, while Lairds' men completed various jobs that were better not done within sight of Yankee spies - or Government officials, since, Britain being neutral, the whole transaction was intensely illegal. She also took on board Captain Raphael Semmes and his officers. Some of the Liverpudlian 'delivery crew', probably anticipating prize earnings, stayed with Semmes when he set off on his cruise of destruction.

And what a cruise it was: *Alabama* was probably the most effective commerce raider of all time, capturing or destroying 64 vessels and cargoes representing some $5.2 million. This was not really down to the qualities of the vessel. It was not armoured, or indeed even particularly heavily constructed, nor very heavily armed – her broadside was a modest 4 X 32 pounders, (i.e. 8 in all), but it was augmented by one 68-pounder and a formidable Blakely rifled 100 lb.

She had a reasonable turn of speed, but no more: her barqentine rig allowed her to sail about 10 knots in favourable weather, and using her auxiliary steam propulsion as well she could manage about 11.5 knots. She would have been left gasping for steam had she tried to intercept one of the specialist blockade runners being built to pierce the Yankee blockade, for which the entry level was about 15 knots, and the good ones did far more than that. What was special about *Alabama* was not a matter of coal, cordage, wood or iron: it was quite simply that she had a genius for a captain. 'Jab and move' boxing coaches used to yell at their charges, and Semmes was supremely good at doing just that. What tilted the scales in his favour was that there was far more 'somewhere else' in the Atlantic Ocean, where he could be by the time news of his latest attack was known, than there is in a boxing ring.

Because many of the ports in the world were closed to him, it was always likely that he would run out of coal, stores, fresh water, some other necessity, or luck. Every day of the 22 months he remained at sea without drydocking, the deteriorating condition of the copper sheathing of *Alabama's* hull slowed her by a little more and every day the condition of his ammunition deteriorated a little more. The end was inevitable (see overleaf) but the talents of her captain delayed its coming for a long time.

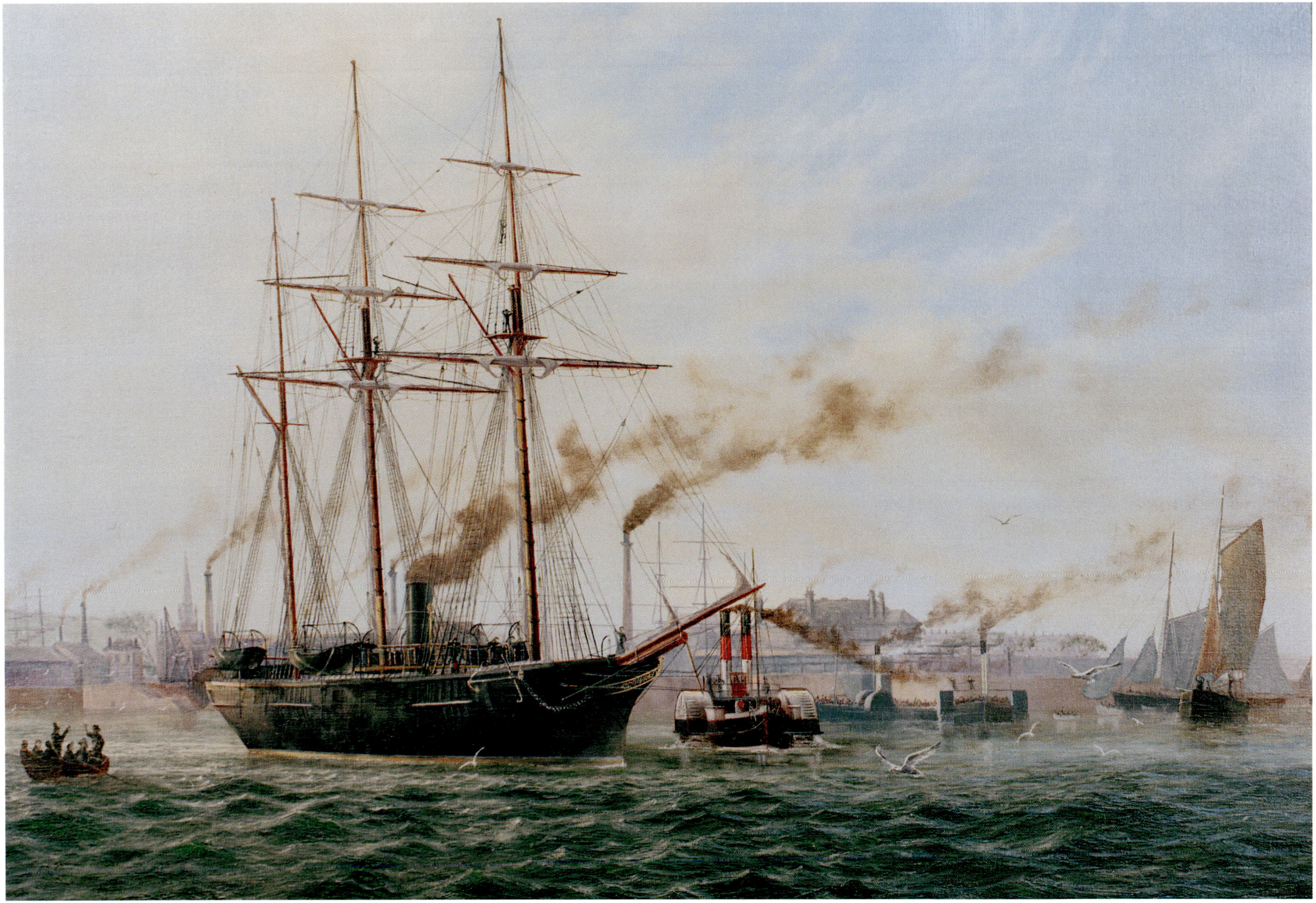

Duel between CSS *Alabama* and USS *Kearsarge*

It was explained (on page 62) how Captain Semmes and the *Alabama* must eventually get caught and sunk. On 11 June 1864, he put into Cherbourg in search of anything the French would supply - water, victuals, stores, coal, drydocking. His shopping list was a long one and some of these were necessities without which he could scarcely continue.

USS *Kearsarge* now arrived on the scene: she was a slightly more powerful ship than Alabama even before the latter's problems were taken into account, but on Sunday 19 June 1864, Semmes left harbour to face her nevertheless. The outcome was what one might expect: *Alabama* scored a few hits initially before the superior discipline and damage control of a properly trained professional warship crew ground the comparatively amateur opposition down. *Alabama's* gunners lost their nerve, firing as soon as the guns were re-loaded, resulting in poor aiming. They also suffered one cruel piece of luck in that a shell from their heavy Blakely gun struck *Kearsarge* what should have been a mortal blow – had it exploded, which it did not. But, inevitably, the *Alabama* continued to ship heavy punishment, and around mid-day she sank.

At this point a new controversy was to break out. In the background of this painting is a steam yacht named *Deerhound*, whose owner, John Lancaster, was aboard. It appeared that he and a few 'Yachtie' friends had put out from Cherbourg to watch the spectacle. However, as *Alabama* sank, *Deerhound* steamed up to her and rescued Semmes, all his officers and quite a lot of his men. When Captain Winslow of the *Kearsarge* signalled to thank Mr Lancaster for his humane action and to ask him to hand over the 'prisoners', Lancaster ordered departure at a speed several knots beyond anything *Kearsarge* could manage, later landing his 'guests' at Southampton. Captain Winslow alleged that this had been a pre-meditated rescue mission, while Mr Lancaster maintained that Winslow had continued firing after Semmes struck his colours and made no move to rescue *Alabama's* men, causing him to fear for their safety, and that he, Lancaster, had 'just happened' to be in Cherbourg while on passage home from a cruise.

There is some evidence that the Laird-built *Deerhound* was capable of 20 knots, which would put her in the fastest handful of vessels afloat at the time. Not only is that a fortunate 'just happening', in addition to being a member of the Royal Yacht Squadron, Lancaster was also a member of the Royal Mersey Yacht Club, where his fellow-members included quite a few Liverpool cotton merchants, and we know where their sympathies would lie. The issue is given an extra twist when we ask whether, if *Deerhound* was simply acting as a floating grandstand, her engineer would have kept up the full head of steam necessary for her precipitate exit. Might he not have left her in light steam and gone up on the after deck to watch the battle too?

Be that as it may, the 'prisoners' lived to fight another day. After such tales of derring-do, it is a shame that Semmes should have chosen to use his memoirs to record a lot of whingeing along the lines 'we wuz robbed'. His astonishing success prior to the final battle deserved a more magnanimous reaction to his eventual and inevitable defeat. One might otherwise have deemed him a great naval figure.

As for the ship, she has remained controversial, in death as in life. When the wreck was discovered there were ideas of raising it in whole or in part, but to whom did it belong? When sunk, the vessel had been in international waters, but by the time she was found French territorial waters had been extended such that she now lay within them. The United States re-asserted ownership with the CSS *Alabama* Preservation Act 1989 and there, for the time being, the matter rests.

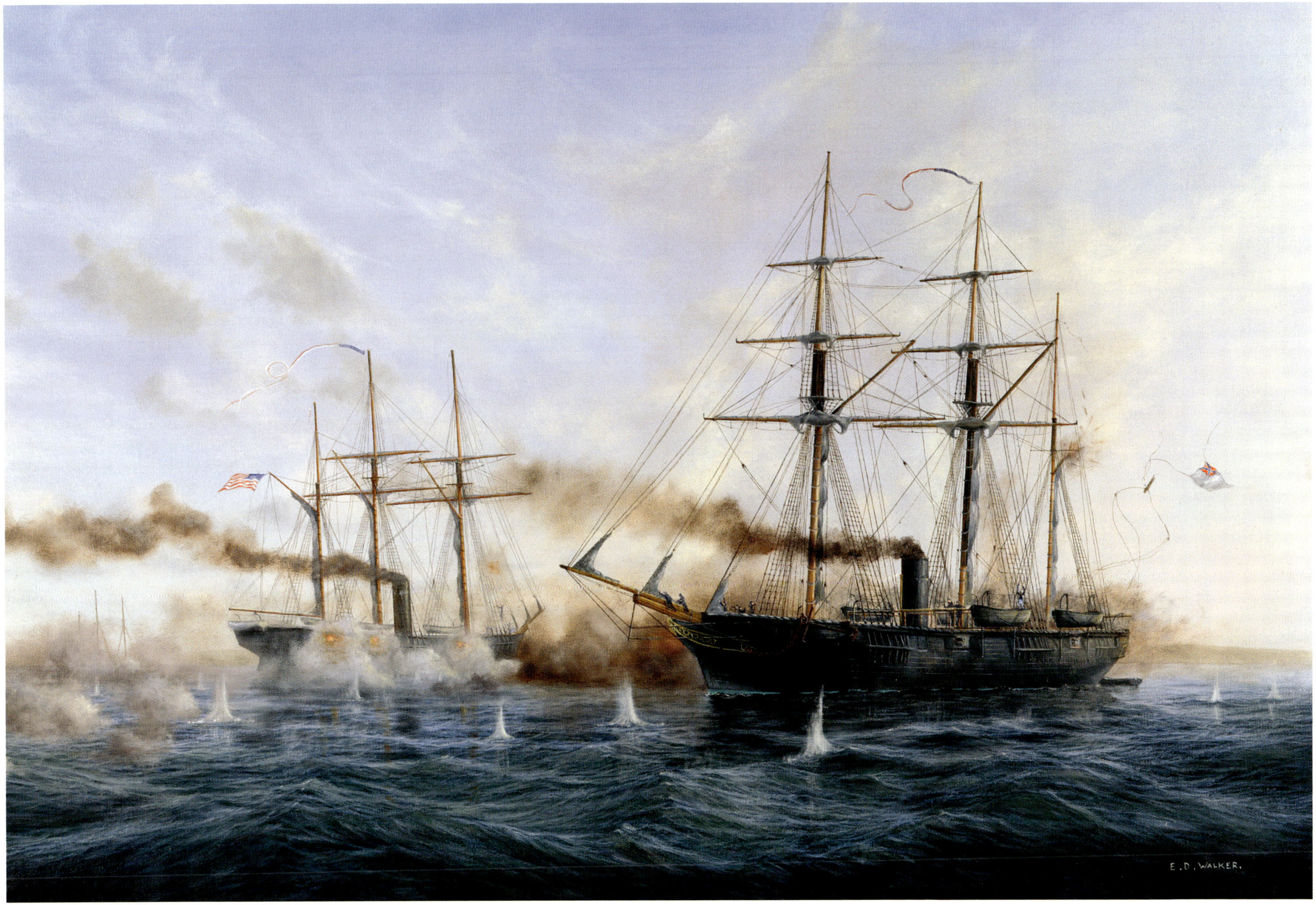
E.D. WALKER.

CSS *Shenandoah* entering the Mersey, off Perch Rock

The sinking of the CSS *Alabama* created a procurement problem for Bulloch. The Union agents in Liverpool and Birkenhead were highly likely to prevent the delivery of any more purpose-built warships (as they did with the two ironclad ram steamers built by Laird's) and in any case, he needed tonnage in a hurry. He therefore purchased a fast three masted full-rigged ship with auxiliary steam power and a lifting screw, named *Sea King*. She was 222 ft long, 1,152 tons and her engines were of 200 nhp. He had her take on all her 'innocent' stores and equipment at Liverpool, before clearing for Bombay and the East Indies. Meanwhile, his other recent purchase, a fast blockade-runner named *Laurel*, was loading guns and ammunition in London. The crew of *Sea King* were somewhat surprised when they arrived in Funchal (Madeira) and rendezvoused with *Laurel* at a nearby uninhabited island named Las Desertas, and within two days the essentials of arming the vessel, now re-named CSS *Shenandoah*, were completed. She carried four 8″ smooth-bore guns, two Whitworth 32-pounder rifled guns and two 12-pounders. Overall, she was at least as capable a raider as *Alabama* had been and was said to have been an ideal vessel to 'swoop' on whalers.

Initially, her Captain, James Waddell, had a problem, because when his crew discovered that they were not bound for Bombay, only 23 out of 80 men on board were willing to stay with the ship. Fortunately for him, these included 19 commissioned or warrant Confederate Navy officers who were able to serve as a cadre around which 'volunteers' from among the crews of the prizes he took could be formed into an adequate crew.

He effectively commenced hostilities in November 1864 and between then and June 1865 he took or destroyed 38 vessels. That does not sound very many compared with the Alabama's 64, but in value terms, *Alabama* did damage to Union vessels to the tune of up to $6,547,609. *Shenandoah* did only about $60,000 less in a significantly shorter time and did not end by getting sunk. This monetary success was a result of the decision to target the Union whaling industry, which was both extremely valuable to the North and extremely susceptible to attack by *Shenandoah*. Another measure of her success is that the South had at various times nine other commerce raiders whose total booty amounted to about $4,000,000.

The story behind these two paintings is stranger than that, indeed some might think stranger than fiction. Unaware that the war had ended in April, Waddell carried on cruising in the vicinity of the Bering Straits, destroying a number of whalers before he finally 'spoke with' the British barque *Barracouta* on August 2 and learned of the embarrassing position he was in: some two thirds of his victims had been taken in peacetime! If he went to a neutral port in the hope that the fuss would die down, the chances were that he would be tracked down and tried for piracy. If he went and surrendered in a US port it was almost certain he would be tried, found guilty and executed. Where in the world could he go, having dismounted his guns, to surrender and get on with the rest of his life? He made up his mind, and sailed 17,000 miles to Liverpool, arriving on 6 November. During the whole of that epic voyage he did not 'speak' with another vessel. He surrendered to Captain Paynter, of the Mersey guardship HMS *Donegal*, who arrested Waddell, the vessel and his crew and put a prize crew aboard, pending the return of the vessel to USA. The Confederates were granted an early parole.

C.F. Adams, U.S. Minister to Great Britain 1861-68, raised the piracy issue, but the British government was not interested. Waddell, by now popularly dubbed 'Rip van Winkle', saw his great gamble pay off.

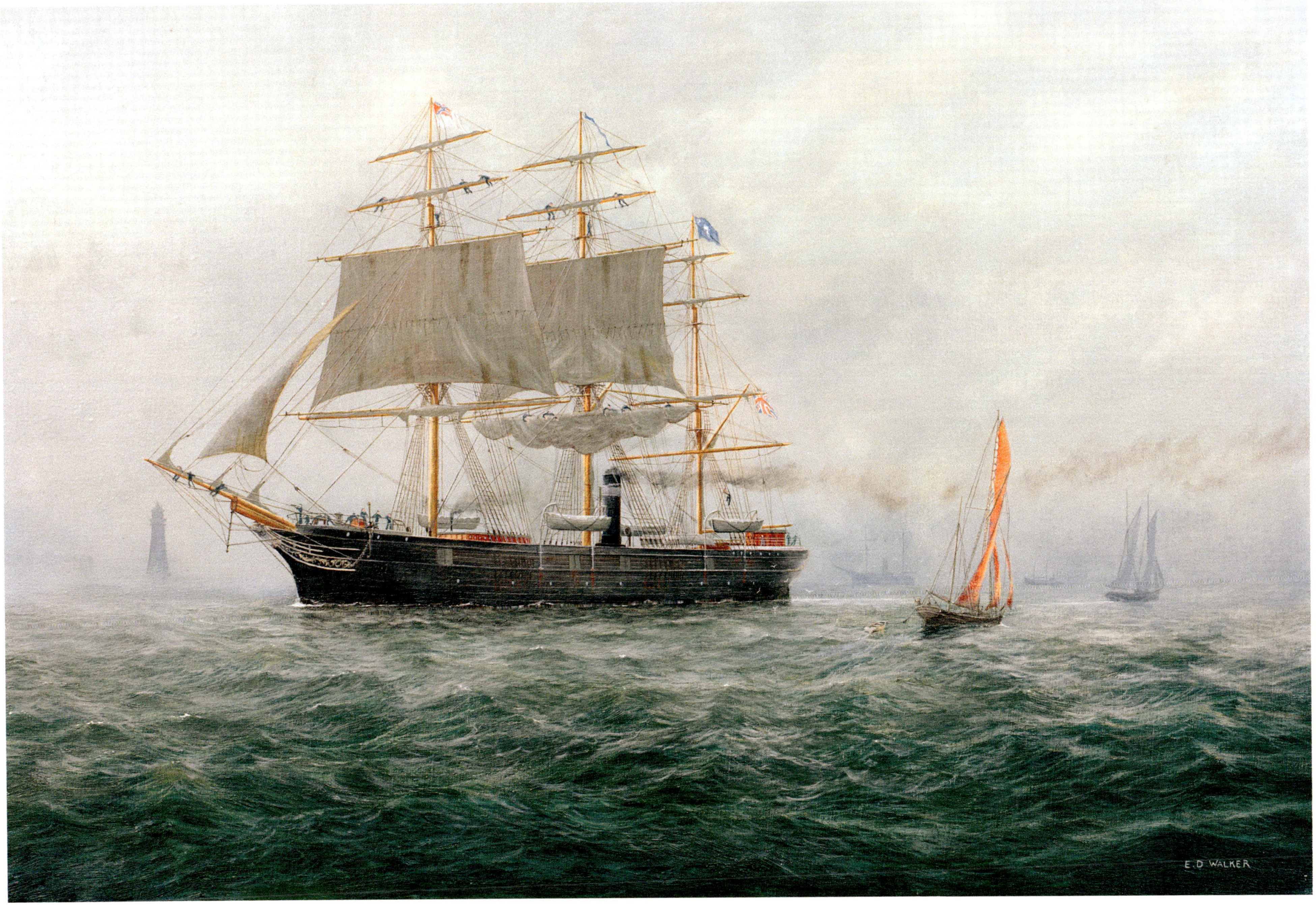
E.D WALKER

CSS *Shenandoah* surrendering to HMS *Donegal* in the Mersey

Although it is not very 'politically correct' to approve of the Confederacy, it is perhaps permissible to draw attention to the part Liverpool played in the American Civil War, which was the fundamental reason why 'Rip van Winkle' made his amazing voyage to safety. At bottom, the Southern States dominated American cotton production, American cotton dominated British cotton imports through Liverpool, which dominated cotton spinning in Lancashire, then still the largest industry the world had seen to date. The stakes were high, and both the Confederacy and the Liverpool cotton merchants and traders knew it.

The Confederacy had arranged for Charles Prioleau to act as their banker in Liverpool, and the largest single demand on his funds was the warships ordered by Bulloch. In all, he ordered twelve warships, of which seven were seized by the British and French governments. Three of those were ironclad steamers with turret-mounted main armament, to be built at Laird's Birkenhead yard: the Union's navy was still made up largely of wooden sailing ships, among which these vessels would have caused mayhem.

The local connection did not end with warship building. While the Union blockade was in position but not impenetrable there would be those who sought to penetrate it in order to benefit from the high market price of raw cotton in Liverpool and the high prices of a wide variety of manufactured goods, including weapons, in the South. One common mode of operation was to ship goods out to Bermuda in conventional cargo vessels, where they would await transhipment onto a specialist blockade runner. These were low-profile fine-lined cargo vessels vessels built of steel to maximise the usable cargo space within their small hulls, which were almost invariably between 200 and 500 tons. There were at this time two areas which were pre-eminent in the construction of metal hulls and where there were builders who already knew how to build ultra-fast vessels like the *Deerhound* - the Clyde and the Mersey. That both were also areas with strong ties to the cotton trade was fortuitous. Blockade runners were built on both rivers, all of them fast, some of them amazingly so. *Will o' the Wisp*, for example, was said to be capable of 17.5 knots, some 75% faster than a typical warship in the blockade. Liverpool's output was better-known than Glasgow's, largely because the local yard of Jones, Quiggin succeeded in launching five blockade runners in one day, and the Illustrated London News published an engraving of the five of them side by side on the launching ways.

The blockade runners' method was to approach the blockade just as dawn was breaking, when their low, pale grey hulls were hardest to spot, at a point near to one of the Confederate forts on shore. They would then run at maximum speed to get within the protective range of the guns of the fort, after which they could proceed, relatively at leisure, to whichever port they were bound for. At first it was easy, but the Union first managed to stiffen the blockade and then as they enjoyed increasing success on land, they began to capture the coastal forts sometimes from the landward side, sometimes by combined operations. It was one such attack, in January 1865 which resulted in the capture of Fort Fisher, the last surviving fort to protect the blockade runners' approach to Wilmington, and after that, the game was up. There had always been other routes employed, especially that overland via the Mexican port of Matamoros, but Bermuda-Wilmington seems to have been the Liverpool men's favourite.

From at least 1863 it had been a highly risky business, but spectacular profits could be achievable. *Banshee* (I) was taken on her eighth voyage, but had already made her shareholders a profit of 700% on their outlay. With such gains beckoning there would always be people willing to take the risk, especially since it was fairly commonplace for the first voyage to pay off the whole building cost of the vessel, which was typically in the region of £40,000.

Estimates and claims vary widely. This was the sum claimed in compensation from Britain, and is, naturally, higher than some others quoted for other purposes!

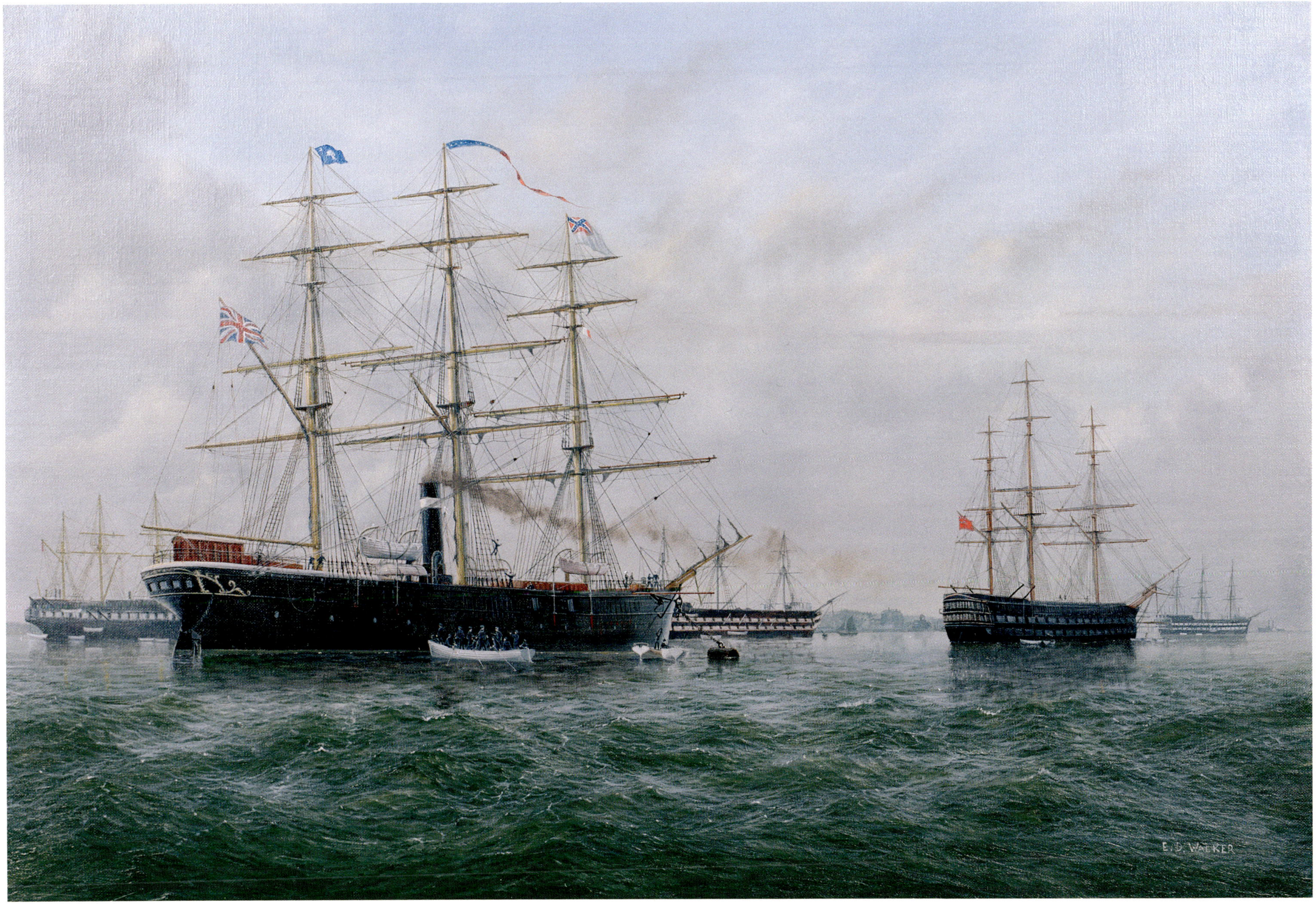
E. D. WALKER

Atlantic Convoy: Corvette escorting WW2 Convoy During the Battle of the Atlantic

The Battle of the Atlantic was the longest and probably the bloodiest engagement of the Second World War and in it the Merchant Navy suffered greater per capita losses than did any of the armed forces. Germany's High Seas Fleet of the Great War had been surrendered in toto under the terms of the Treaty of Versailles which ended the Great War, though in one last act of defiance its ships were scuppered in Scapa Flow. The Third Reich's navy was designed on different principles. Two mighty battleships and two formidable battlecruisers were backed by three so-called pocket battleships, two heavy cruisers, a larger number of light cruisers and destroyers and many submarines. Such a navy could not engage in a major battle, nor was it intended to. The large surface units were intended to be 'a fleet in being' so that the Allied fleets had to deploy large forces simply to keep tabs on them. But they also knew that in 1917, U-boats had brought Britain to within a few weeks of really serious food shortage and that the British surface blockade of Germany had produced terrible hardship for the civilian population.

None of the German surface units actually did much damage to merchant shipping when compared with that done by submarines and aircraft, and by 1942, with some sunk and others bottled up in port, the Nazi surface navy could be considered virtually a spent force. This meant that it was no longer necessary for allied convoy escorts to include heavy units to confront them, and little vessels like the Flower class corvette shown here could not just join in, but bear the brunt of escort duties. The 'Flowers' were designed by Smith's Dock Company of Middlesborough, and first built in 1939, based on a whale-catcher design which could be quickly and cheaply produced, often in very small shipyards, of which you or I have never heard. They used triple expansion reciprocating engines, long out of date, but capable of being built in old-fashioned yards which had contacts with little old-fashioned foundries. On the cinder floors of out-dated yards were built some 150 little warships which would become winners. As the threat of long-range aircraft deployed from occupied France grew, they were supplemented by other relatively little ships like the *Cairo* and *Black Swan* classes of specialist anti-aircraft vessels.

Much of the winning of the Battle of the Atlantic happened in Liverpool, in two ways. The first was the establishment of Western Approaches Command which co-ordinated the movements of merchant and naval forces, with its associated training school, and the second was the development of the 'support group', exemplified by the successes of the legendary Captain Johnny Walker. At the beginning of the campaign, escorts had to defend their convoys reactively: Johnny Walker had the good fortune to have enough ships to divide convoy escorts into close escorts which stayed with the merchantmen and 'support groups' which mounted pre-emptive counter-attacks on the fringes of the convoys. It was on the cheapness and 'buildability' of such as the Flower class that this development depended, and these – let's be blunt – cramped, uncomfortable and often scruffy little ships, were the real victors to whom Grand Admiral Doenitz surrendered when the U-Boat campaign in the North Atlantic was abandoned in May 1943.

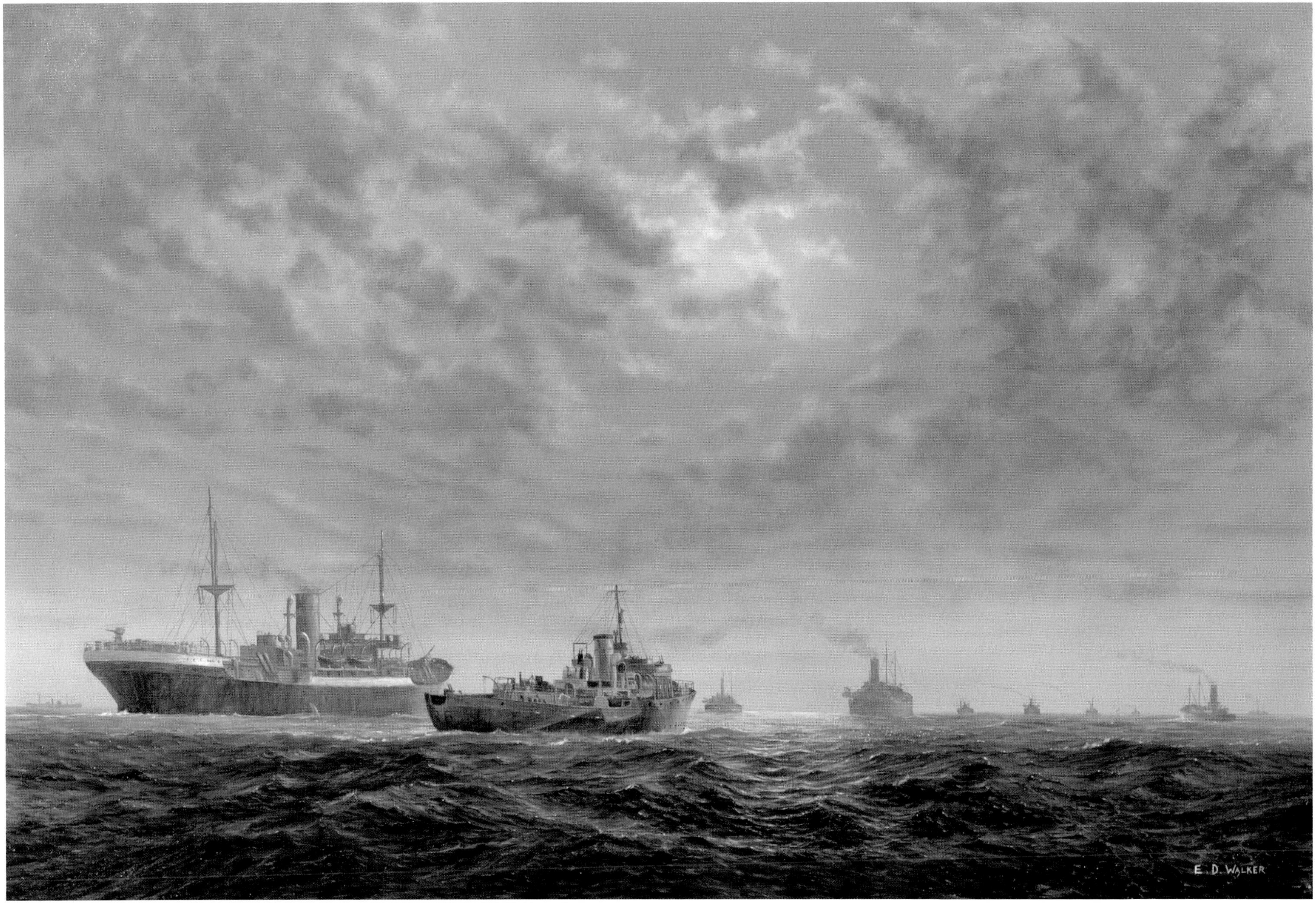
E. D. WALKER

HMS *Whimbrel*

Like the Flower class corvettes, *Black Swan* class sloops were purpose-built convoy escorts and HMS *Whimbrel,* commissioned in 1943, is a modified *Black Swan.* They had something of the 'buildability' of the Flower class, but were much larger and more powerful vessels. Thanks to the conspicuous successes of Captain Johnny Walker, of HMS *Starling,* they became best known as anti-submarine vessels, but were designed as anti-aircraft vessels, for which role they were well-equipped. They mounted three twin 4-inch high angle turrets for longer ranges, two twin 40mm Bofors for closer ranges and two twin and two single 20mm Oerlikons for really close range. They had stabilisers to make them steadier gun-platforms when engaging aircraft and were fitted with depth charge rails and throwers.

Whimbrel was built at Glasgow, and is 299ft 6in long, displacing 1,350 tons. She had accommodation for eight officers and 200 other ranks, and her Parsons steam turbines produced 4,300 shp, giving over 18 knots. 29 of the 'modified' class were built between 1942 and 1946.

Whimbrel's first duties were at the anti-submarine training school at Tobermory, Isle of Mull, before she joined Captain Walker's near-legendary 2nd Support Group. She left Liverpool for Gibraltar and then went for refitting at Hartlepool, until February 1944, when she rejoined the 2nd Support Group. The submarine threat having been withdrawn from the North Atlantic, the Group was 'lent' to the Home Fleet and *Whimbrel,* escorted Arctic convoys carrying war supplies to Murmansk. Then she was back to Liverpool for refitting before escort duties on the supply lines of the Allied forces during and after D-day. More modernisation work followed, this time at Newport, then she was off to the Far East, arriving shortly before VE day to spend the rest of the war escorting fleet tankers. It was a potentially risky job, but in fact she never engaged an enemy vessel during those last months of the war.

Her '15 minutes of fame' came when, along with her sister HMS Crane, she was part of the Royal Navy's presence in Tokyo Bay on 2 September 1945, the occasion of the Japanese surrender. But when her 15 minutes were up. she was unceremoniously booted into reserve in June 1947. Two years later, she was sold to the Egyptian Navy for about £247,000.

Whimbrel needed a new name, and became *El Marek Farouk* and was re-named again as *Tariq.* She served through the Suez crisis, surviving an attack by French carrier-based aircraft. *Tariq* continued in active service in the various conflicts in the region, but by 1980 she was of very limited combat value and was chiefly deployed as a training and accommodation vessel. Even so, she continued to go to sea until 1997.

The attentive reader will have noticed that, where appropriate, *Whimbrel* is referred to in the present tense. She still exists and is in remarkably good condition for a vessel of her age. She is the only survivor of the hundreds of convoy escort craft and remains comparatively un-modernised since 1946, She is a monument to the greatest sea battle that this sea-faring nation has ever fought. She is a monument not just to the little convoy escort ships based in Canning Dock or Gladstone Dock but also to the organisation set up by Sir Percy Noble and his successor Sir Peter Gretton, in Western Approaches Command which enabled them to move from fairly hopeless reactive responses to the U-boat menace to highly confident pro-active ones, of which the most successful were the 'support groups' in which *Whimbrel* sailed. She is a monument to men like Captain Johnny Walker, who may have spent their hours afloat in deeds of derring-do but spent their time ashore in devising and disseminating tactics which would account overall for nearly 1,000 Axis submarines. They would also secure Britain's food and fuel supplies.

Britain has preserved remarkably few of the warships which built and defended its Empire. We have HMS *Victory,* but that is not a preserved warship, it is a holy shrine to 'the blessed memory'. We have HMS *Warrior,* which was a world-beating piece of technology but never fired her guns in anger. The nearest we have to a 'big gun' ship is HMS *Belfast,* admittedly a very handsome vessel, but are 6in. guns 'big guns'? Above all, however, we need a little ship. The convoy escort craft saved Britain from collapse in 1942 and won a famous victory in 1943. *Whimbrel* is the only remaining chance to provide a substantial monument to those desperate years.

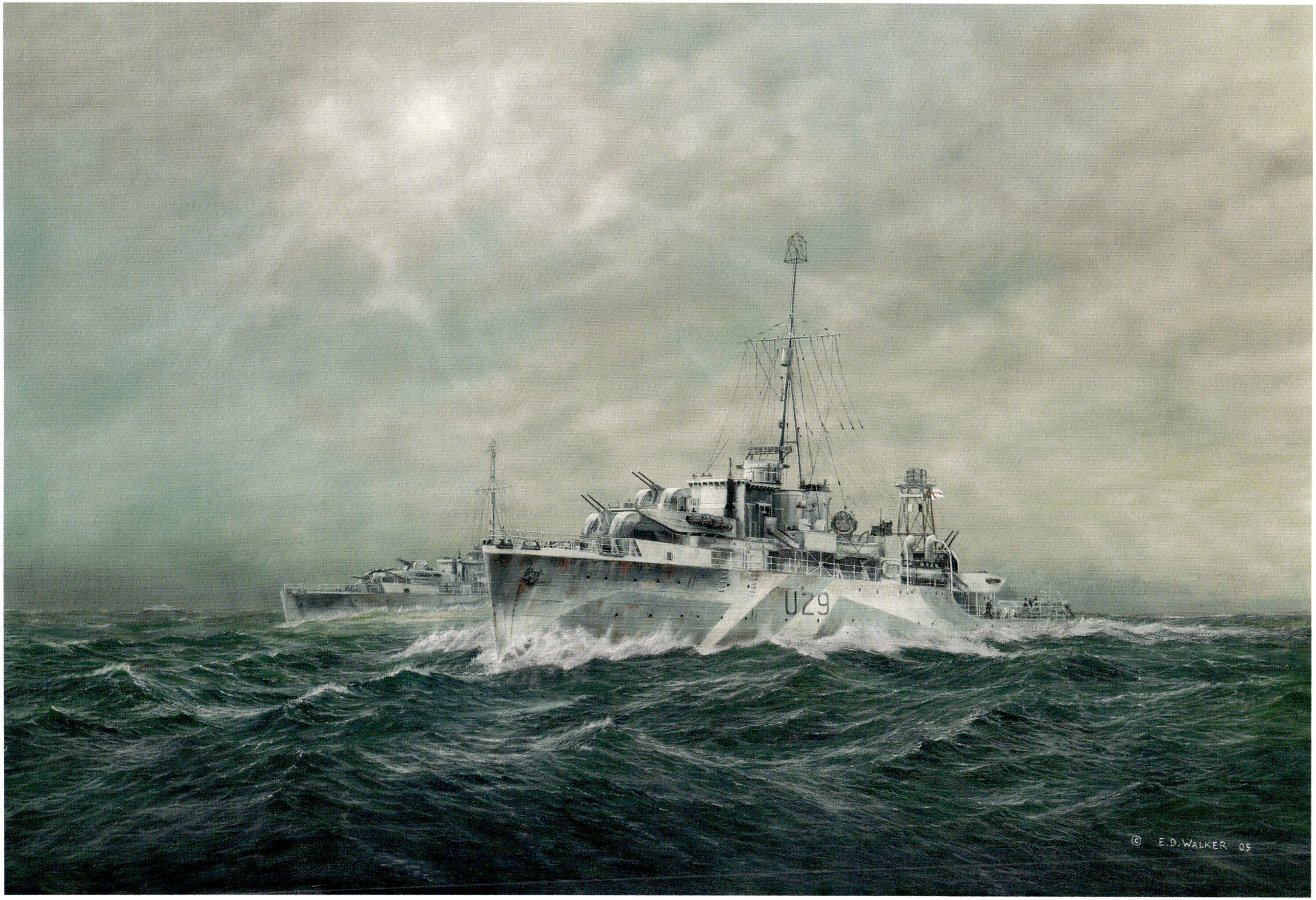
U29
© E.D.WALKER 05

HMS *Unicorn* Leaving Laird's: Laird's last ship

William Laird was one of a number of businessmen interested in founding an independent port in Birkenhead and, having purchased some land on the banks of Wallasey Pool, he began business there as a boilermaker in 1824 in partnership with Daniel Horton. This partnership lasted only until 1828, when William's son John joined the business, henceforth known as William Laird & Son.

From the start, the firm's output was almost exclusively of iron steamers, which was the right market sector to be in at that time, and its first screw-propelled vessel was as early as 1838. This was the new technology, and Laird's prospered by supplying it. They soon moved into warship construction, with vessels for the East India Company and in 1845 launched the Royal Navy's first iron frigate, the ill-fated *Birkenhead*. The growth of business and the gradual construction of Birkenhead docks required a change of premises, and in 1857 the 'New Yard' was opened just south of Woodside.

The physical appearance of most of the extent of the yards at the time of *Unicorn's* commissioning in 1993 was determined by two developments: in 1901 the Mersey Docks & Harbour Board began reclaiming Tranmere Bay, which would be occupied by a shipyard developed by a new company which was, in effect, Laird Bros., in disguise. In 1903, Laird's amalgamated with Charles Cammell & Co, steel manufacturers. The 'new yard' and the even newer yard existed side by side, resulting in some organisational problems but by the time business began to pick up after the two mini-slumps of the Edwardian years, Laird's were well placed to benefit, and then spent the war years and the brief post-war boom working to full capacity. They were relatively successful in gaining warship contracts in the inter-war years and were phenomenally busy during the war and afterwards. But in the fifties it started to become clear that the once-dominant British shipbuilding industry was simply not competitive in a world market. This prompted investment at Laird's to allow indoor pre-fabrication of large sub-assemblies, and this was followed by the construction of the huge covered construction hall which dominates the site today. All was to no avail: privatised in 1986, the yard was incorporated into Vickers of Barrow, which decided that in future Barrow would build nuclear submarines and Birkenhead diesel-electric ones.

HMS *Unicorn*, commissioned in 1993, was the last of four Upholder class submarines, of which three were built at Laird's. They displaced 2,455 tons submerged and their diesel-electric machinery would drive them at 12 knots surfaced or 'snorting' or 20 knots submerged. They were armed with ship-to-ship missiles and homing torpedoes and, at the expense of leaving their torpedoes behind, could also lay mines. The ship's complement was 47.

The four ships were delivered nicely in time for the defence cuts of the so-called 'peace dividend' after the Cold War ended: they were withdrawn in 1994 and sold to the Canadian Navy in 1998. They were overhauled and re-commissioned at Barrow and *Unicorn*, now HMCS *Windsor*, was finally handed over to her new owners in 2001. A government decision to build no more diesel-electric submarines had already been taken before these unfortunate vessels were completed, which spelled the end for a famous old firm.

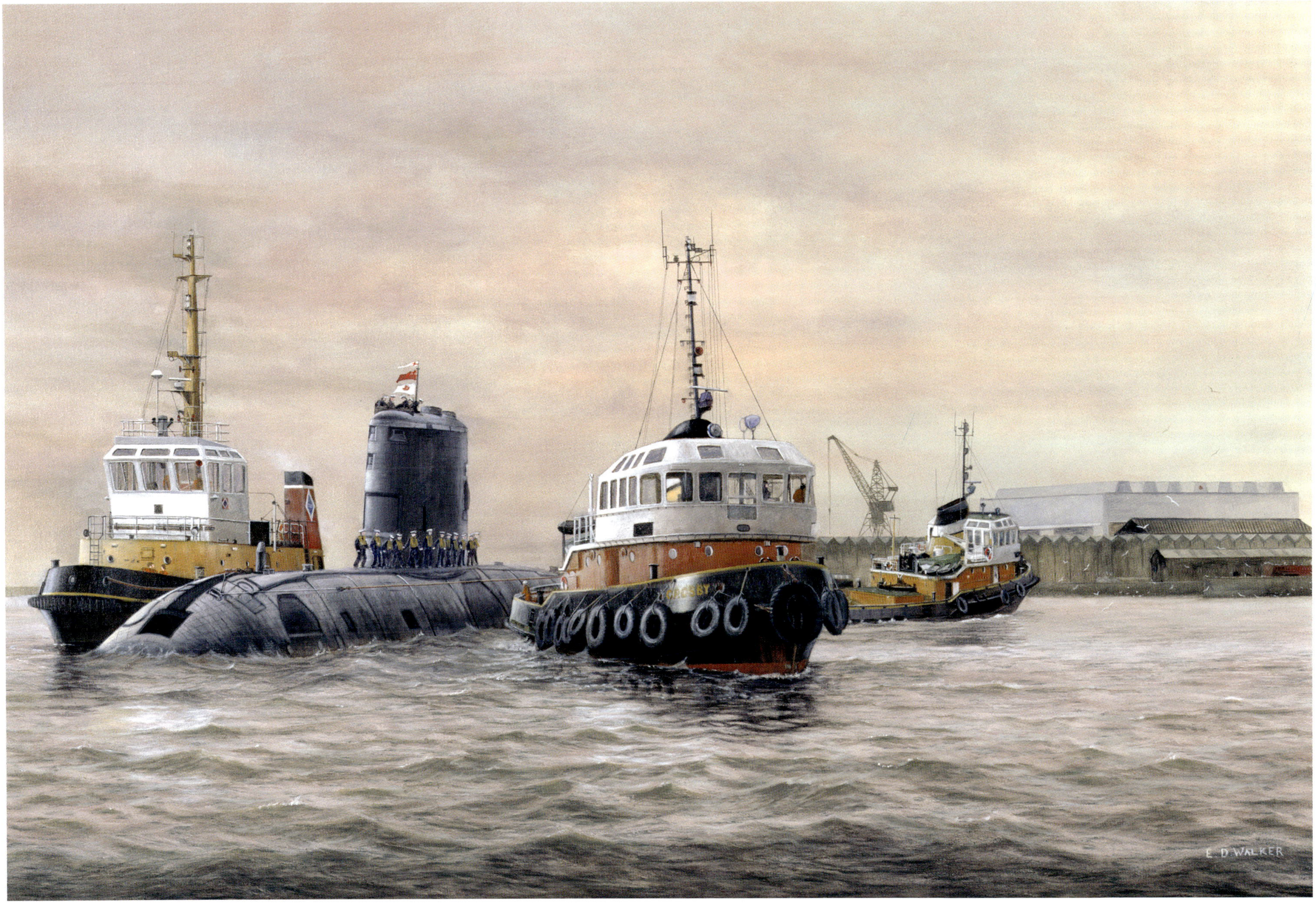

CROSBY
E. D. WALKER

HMS *Cornwall*

In May 1943, following mounting and unsustainable losses at the hands of surface escorts, long-range aircraft, and escort carrier aircraft, the German submarine campaign in the North Atlantic was ended. This removed probably the most serious threat Britain had faced in the earlier part of the war, and formed a significant pointer to eventual victory. 1993 saw a great commemoration of the event, centred, like the anti-submarine campaign itself, in Liverpool and Bootle. On 26 May, Prince Philip, on board the Royal Yacht *Britannia*, reviewed a mixed fleet of over 40 naval and merchant vessels of the former combatant nations in Moelfre Bay, Anglesey. It was an unforgettable occasion for those present, not least because of absolutely vile weather. One of the stars of the show was HMS *Cornwall*, which was fleet flagship for the event.

She is one of the third batch of *Broadsword*-class frigates (Type 22) and was built at Glasgow by Yarrow, entering commission in 1988. Her full-load displacement is 4,900 tons and her Rolls Royce gas turbines will take her up to 30 knots. Armed with Harpoon ship-to-ship and Sea Wolf ship-to-air guided missiles and with homing torpedoes, her anti-aircraft defences are more powerful than those of *Broadsword* as built: experience in the Falklands conflict led to the addition of two 30mm quick-firing cannon and the formidable 'Goalkeeper' short-range system. What Falkland experience did nothing to change was the retention of the 4.5 inch turret-mounted gun, whose high rate of fire makes up for its rather puny appearance. The helicopter hangar can carry either two Lynx helicopters or one Sea King and the ship's complement is 250.

The painting shows her leaving the moorings which had been specially laid for her: she was to be in pride of place just off Albert Dock, which gives visitors a marvellous view of visiting vessels, but is unfortunately not good 'holding ground' for ships' anchors. This is a matter of some importance where five-knot tides are pretty commonplace and seven knots is not unknown. These moorings were left in, ready for the visit of *Queen Elizabeth 2* the following year. At 0930 pm Thursday 27th, the Royal Yacht arrived at the Floating Stage. The highlights of the following day included Her Majesty the Queen's inspection of the Royal Guard, her opening of the Merseyside Maritime Museum and her meeting with Battle of the Atlantic veterans in Bootle.

There were many other events, including a commemorative service for which even the huge space of Liverpool Cathedral could not accommodate anywhere near all the people who wanted to go, parades, re-unions, receptions, dinners and an international historical conference.

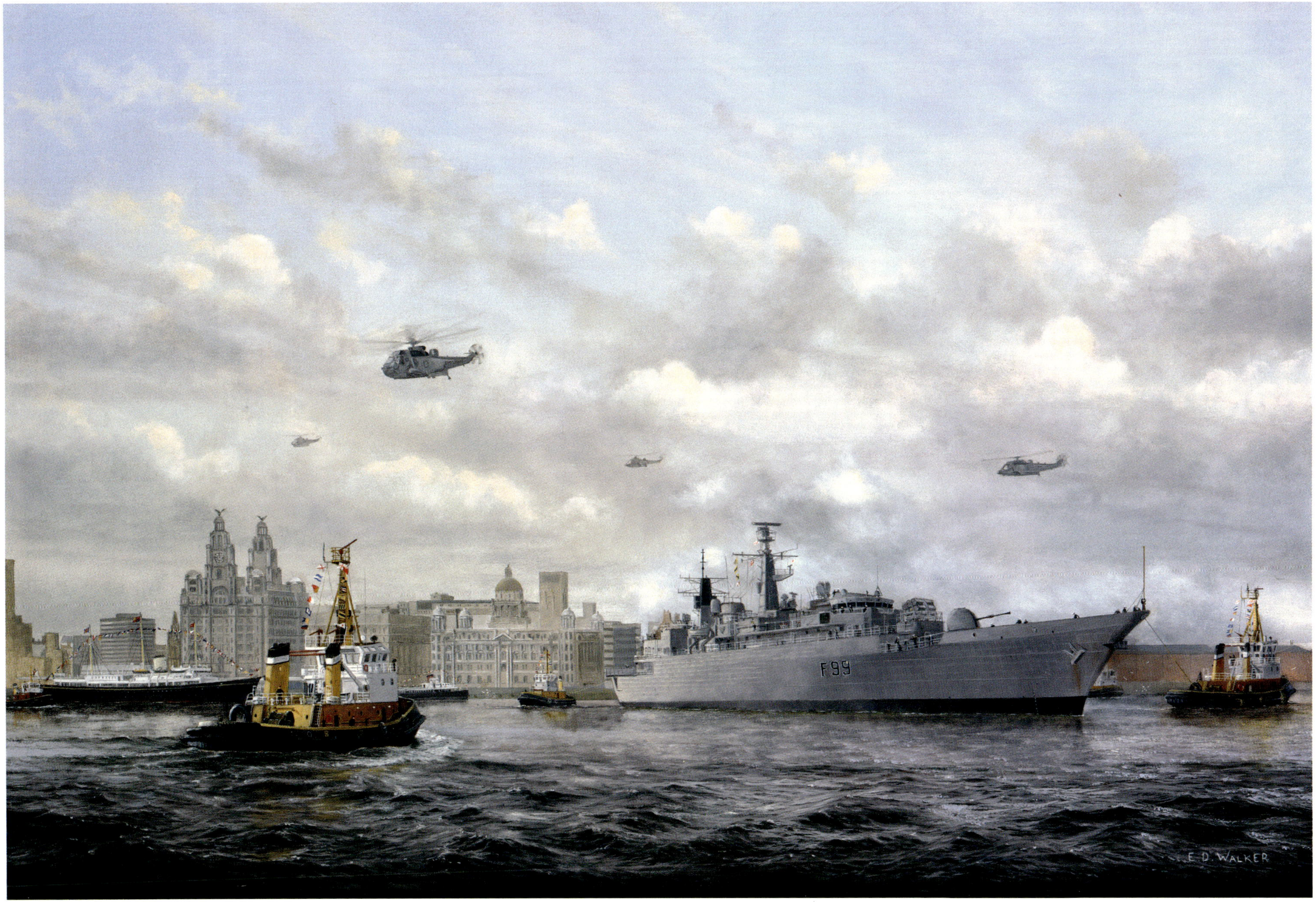
F99
E. D. WALKER

Liverpool Pilot Schooner Number 2, *Leader*, built 1856

The provision of port pilotage in Liverpool evolved from a situation where an incoming skipper hired a local fisherman to see him safely through the the tortuous approach channels to the Mersey. This 'system', if such one could call it, was marginally formalised by an Act of 1766, but in one crucial respect the pilotage service did not change until the 1883: the boats, by then twelve in number, were owned and operated by the pilots, not by the Mersey Docks & Harbour Board. They were incorporated as a department of the Board in 1883 and provided with the splendid building perched on the north edge of the river entrance to Canning Dock and which is now part of the Merseyside Maritime Museum.

The poor availability of the schooners, together with some tragic accidents in an always dangerous activity, helped lead to a complete change of operation: the Pilotage Department was equipped with steamers which acted as floating hotels in which the pilots stayed until it was their turn to board an incoming craft and back to which they were returned by outward bound vessels. The first two steamers were ordered in 1896, and the completion of the conversion came when the last of the sailing boats was sold in 1904.

Pilots long had an evil and largely unjustified reputation among some seafarers for being there to collect dues when you didn't need them and being somewhere else, probably drunk, when you did. This was by no means always a fair judgement, and there were many cases of pilots acting heroically in highly dangerous circumstances, as the story behind this picture illustrates.

On 8 February 1881, the 76ft Pilot Schooner *Leader* was on station in heavy and worsening weather. All around her were ships seeking safety within the river but (rightly) fearful of their chances of finding the channel safely in such weather, which would in any case make the transfer of a pilot to an incoming vessel hazardous if not impossible. The decision taken by the Master Pilot of *Leader* showed a genuine 'Nelson Touch': disregarding every regulation about pilots boarding inward-bound vessels, he hoisted the signal 'Follow me' and twelve vessels followed the course he set, arriving safely in the river.

Merseyside Maritime Museum has a wonderful model of this vessel at 1:12 scale, which was built by her first Master Pilot, Captain Hudson. In 1862 it became the first ship model accessioned by the then Liverpool Museum.

In the early 1980s, the then Government's Job Creation Programme represented an opportunity to take on and train young people in traditional ship and boat-building techniques, taught by older craftsmen, and, at the same time, to provide an enhanced sail training capability. The Liverpool Pilot schooners were well-regarded as fast and handy boats, relatively cheap to build at only 76 feet long, but robust enough to go to sea. *Spirit of Merseyside* was loosely based on *Leader* and was originally intended to be ready for the visit of the Tall Ships to Liverpool in 1984. However, she was not 'launched' (by a mobile crane) until 17 February 1985, and after that a stability problem was encountered, necessitating the replacement of her iron keel weight with a lead one. She ran out of local sponsorship and became *Spirit of Scotland*.

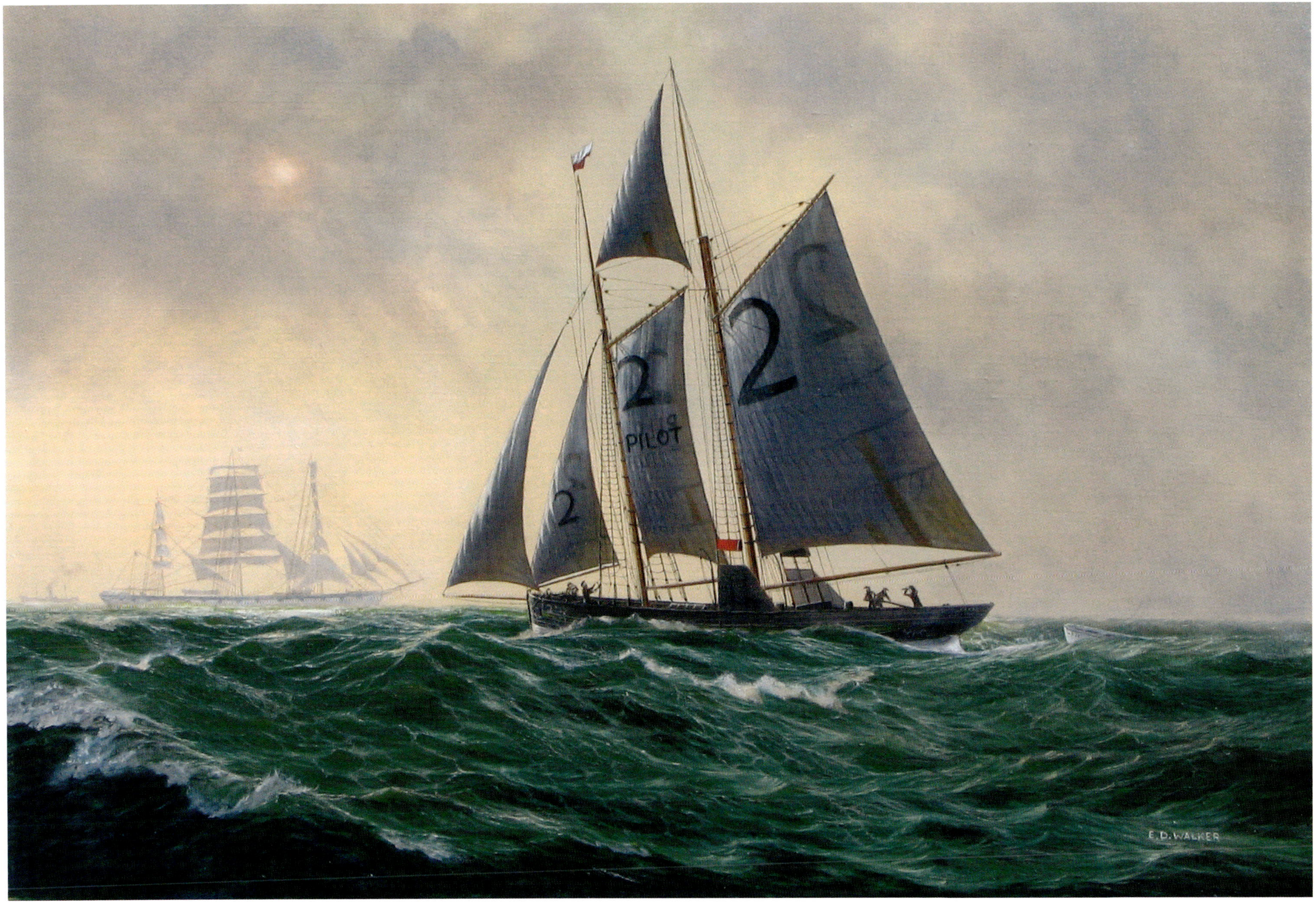
2
2
PILOT
2
E.D. WALKER

Walter J Chambers No 2, 1917

When the pilotage service changed from sail to steam, one thing which did not change was the practice of re-using numbers, so that when *Walter J Chambers* was built to replace *Leonard J Spear No 2*, in 1917, she took over the number with the job, as, indeed more distantly she specified her lineage back to *Leader*. Who was Walter J. Chambers to get a boat named after him? He was, of course, a member of the Mersey Docks & Harbour Board, serving from 1902 to 1929, during the latter part of which time he was Chairman of the Pilotage Committee.

Board policy on such matters was hierarchical: to get a dock named after you, you had to be Board Chairman (eg. Langton, Gladstone). To get a fairly gentlemanly vessel like a pilot boat it was necessary to be a committee chairman, but when you get down to dredgers, mere principal officials could have one (e.g. *Miles K. Burton* or *Lyster*).

To get an important dredger (e.g. *SPD Hugh Crow*) it was still necessary to be an elected member. Nor did the protocol go any further down the line: Principal Assistants to the Engineer-in-Chief could whistle for being immortalised on the bow of a steam hopper barge or a salvage camel – such craft were merely numbered.

The changeover to steam pilot boats resulted in many changes in pilotage practice as well. The 'boats' were in fact substantial little ships. *Walter J Chambers* was 145ft long by 27.7ft wide and measured 479 gross tons. Built by Murdock & Murray of Port Glasgow, she had one triple expansion steam engine of 81 rhp.

The steamers provided accommodation for the pilots. Each had 43 pilots attached to it, of whom at any one time 13 would be ashore to pilot outward vessels and of the remaining thirty, half would be aboard the boat and half off duty.

There were four 'stations' around which the pilot boats cruised: one was off Point Lynas, one between there and the NW lightship and the remaining two between there and the bar. Pilots were transferred by boat to and from the pilot vessel, but because the latter was known as a 'boat' a different name was needed for the small craft, which were known as 'punts'. They were in fact steam, later motor, launches.

Walter J Chambers had a long service life, not being replaced until 1953. Her replacement was the diesel-electric *Edmund Gardner*, built by Philip & Son of Dartmouth and now preserved at Merseyside Maritime Museum. She resembles a tiny passenger liner in the provision of a solarium and a rather splendid dining room for inmates, and the intensely hierarchical social structure which still held the Board in thrall is still visible in her accommodation.

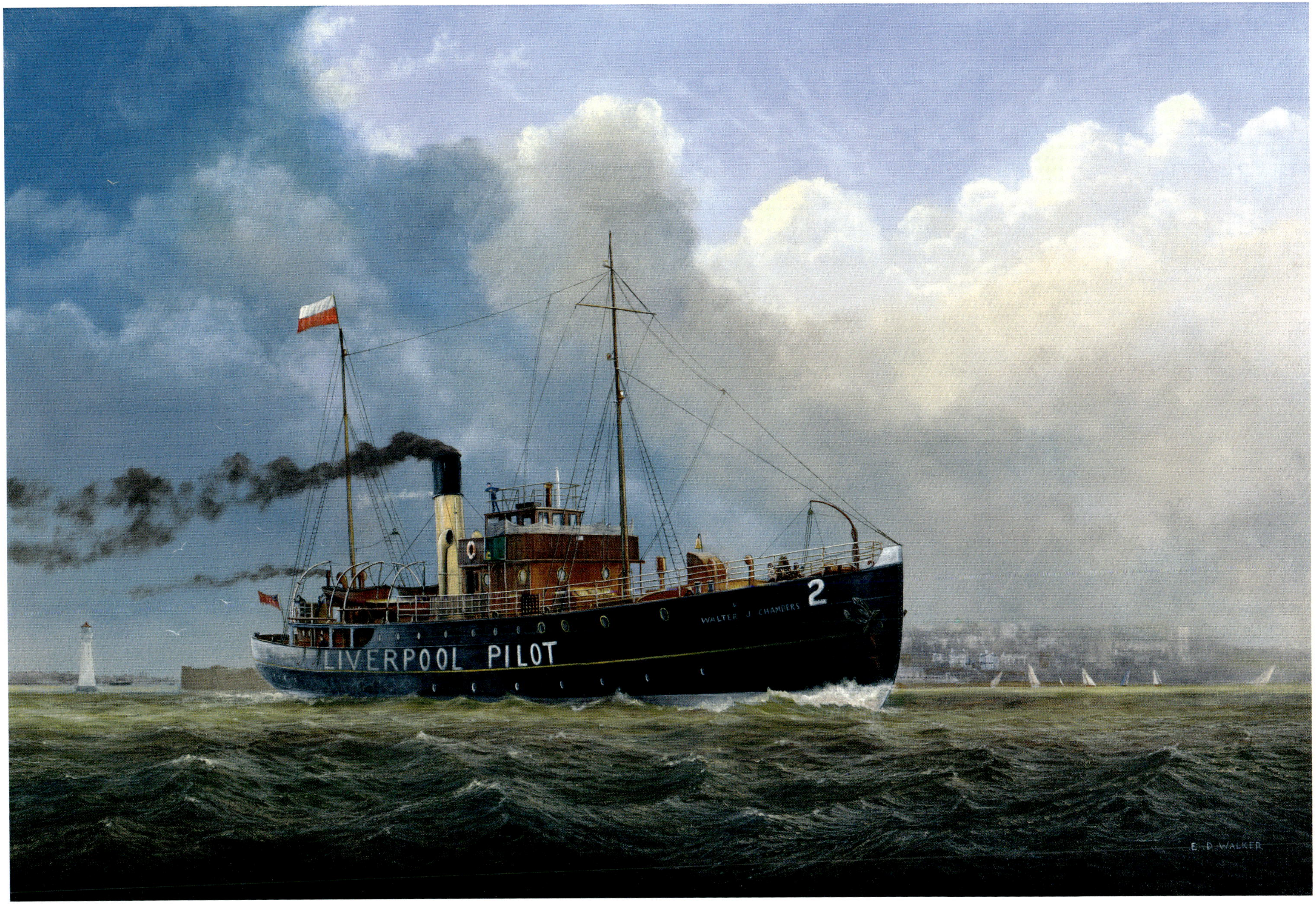
LIVERPOOL PILOT
2
WALTER J. CHAMBERS
E. D. WALKER

Mersey Ferry *Upton*

Upton was one of five new passenger ferries put into service by Birkenhead Corporation between 1925 and 1933, of which four were virtually identical and *Upton* was slightly different. All were built of steel at Cammell Laird's yard, all had twin screws driven by twin triple expansion engines and in all except *Upton* these were of 1,300 indicated horsepower. *Upton's* engines were slightly smaller, reflecting her gross tonnage of 462 as against her half-sisters' tonnages which varied slightly around 485.

The reason for building one of what was effectively a class of five smaller than the others was that she was intended to work the Rock Ferry service, while the others were for the much busier Woodside service. The Rock Ferry service could trace its roots back to about 1660, and in the days before the Wirral roads were turnpiked there was probably much to be said for getting the nearest boat to Liverpool. Its palmy days seem to have been when the roads had been turnpiked, and the Royal Rock Hotel provided for gentlemen to leave horses and/or carriages, or servants, there and go on to Liverpool unencumbered, but it was also the ferry for the mail coaches (whence its Royal appelation).

The opening of the Chester and Birkenhead Railway in 1840 caused the mail coaches to dwindle, until by 1860 there was just a single service to Parkgate and Chester, and that only ran two days a week.

From then on, the Rock Ferry faced a constant struggle to keep going, under a number of different proprietors and lessees until in 1897 it was taken over by Birkenhead Corporation. Within two years, a new pier had been built and an hourly triangular service inaugurated between Rock Ferry, New Ferry and Liverpool. Soon improved to a half-hour service, using two Woodside boats, *Wirral* and *Mersey*, with the little *Firefly* (of only 165 gross tons) which had been acquired along with the route, kept as 'spare'.

The 'South End Ferries', meaning Rock Ferry and New Ferry, carried large numbers of passengers (e.g. 1.9 million in 1908), but consistently lost money: by 1922 the average annual loss was over £20,000. Anticipating the reduced size of *Upton*, they tried a substantially smaller one, the *Storeton* of 1910, which must presumably have been found wanting, since *Upton* was almost 50% larger in gross tonnage.

The Rock Ferry met its inevitable end on 30 June 1939. What remains surprising about the *Upton* is that anyone thought it advisable to build a boat specially for a service whose customer base could fairly be called morbid. Like most Mersey Ferries, she was a good, strongly built little boat and served through the war under requisition, then worked until 1953 with the snappily-branded Southampton, Isle of Wight and South of England Royal Mail Steam Packet Co. Ltd., running summer excursions. She was broken up at Northam.

At Rock Ferry all that remains to remind us of her passing is the original stone jetty. The pier, the stage, the booking office, the Royal Rock Hotel, with its stables, coach houses and servants' vaults outlived the *Upton*, but only by about twenty years.

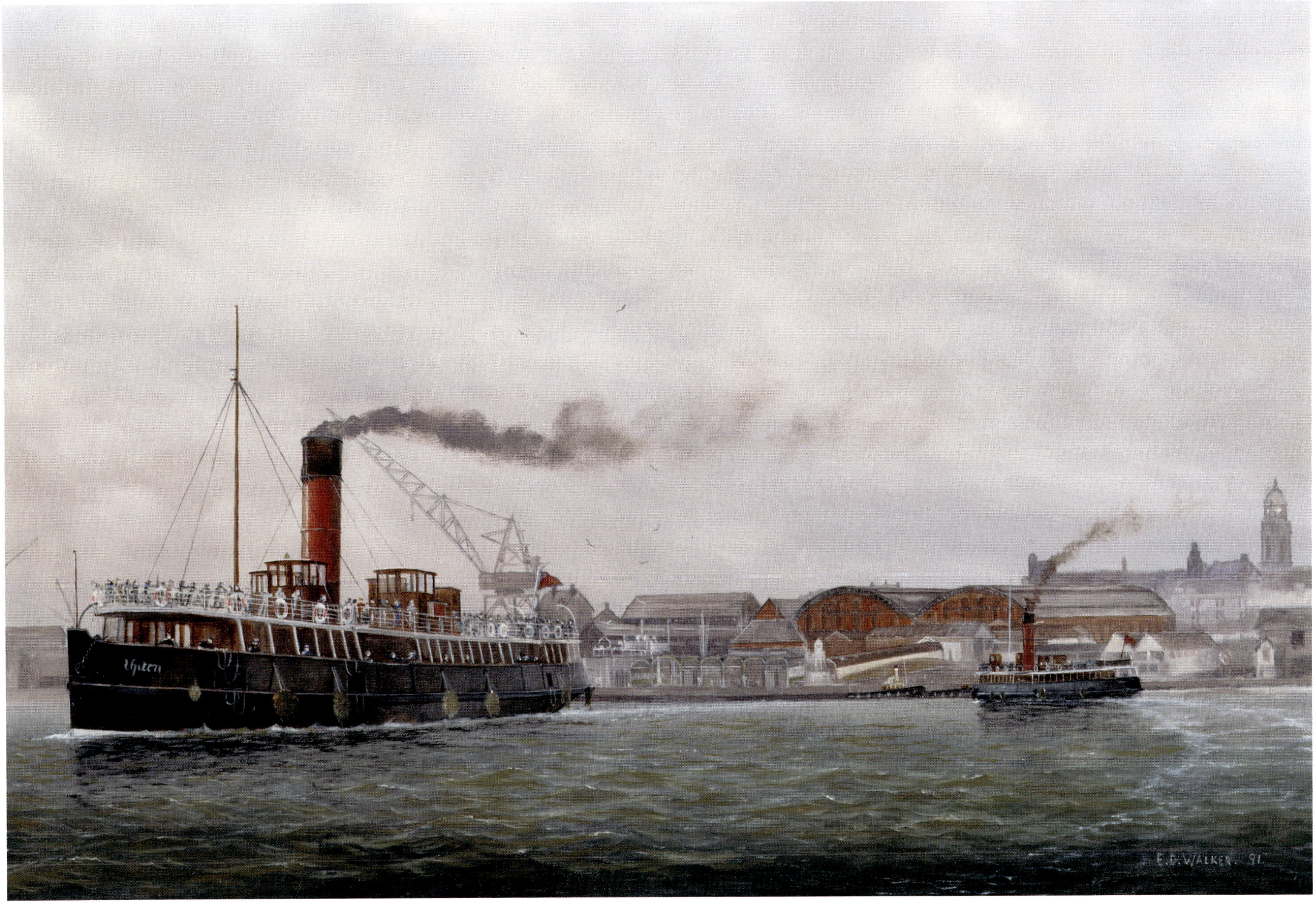
E.D. WALKER '91

Mersey Ferry *Woodchurch*

The Mersey Ferries have a long and tortured history of monastic, private and municipal ownership both of ferry rights and vessels. In the case of the Birkenhead ferries there was also an exceedingly ill-judged sortie into ferry operation by the Birkenhead and Chester Railway as well, in which the Company paid good money for the physical assets of a ferry which had, in fact, no legal rights of ferry.

The pressure exerted on the ferries by railway companies, and especially by the Mersey Railway (which was rather a paper tiger before its electrification in 1903 but a distinctly mean one, red in tooth and claw, thereafter) was bound to force consolidation by the ferries even before the first road tunnel opened in 1934. It was a matter of municipalisation: the numerous ferry undertakings ended up as two Municipal services, the Birkenhead Ferries and the Wallasey Ferries. For the outsider it is a pretty sound rule that if a vessel is named after some village or settlement you might have trouble pointing out on a map it's a Birkenhead boat. If it's named after a flower it's a Wallasey boat. The two municipalities did not like each other very much and were markedly poor at uniting to confront common enemies.

The Birkenhead service was long operated by the four 'half-sisters' of *Upton* (see page 82), but after the war it became increasingly clear that the day of the steam ferry boat was past, and in 1957 Birkenhead Corporation ordered three new diesel propelled vessels, duly named *Mountwood*, *Woodchurch* and *Overchurch*. The first two were built by Philip & Son of Dartmouth, the third by Cammell Laird. (readers might wonder why the Corporation did not place all the business within the borough boundary: Laird's had such a full order book that they were not able to tender for the first two vessels. How things would change!)

The first two vessels entered service in 1960, the third in 1961. Their passenger capacity then was 'about 1,200'. All three are still in service, though modern safety regulations have reduced that 'about 1,200' to various figures, according to minor differences in the boats, in the region of 400-500.

The surviving boats have undergone heavy hull repairs, they have been re-engined and they have new control gear. No matter: they still feel like Mersey Ferries when you ride on one. It's just that, born and brought up in Birkenhead, I gag a bit at them all having been given Wallasey names now. I suppose I might have been even grumpier had *Woodchurch* been re-named *Pansy* instead of *Snowdrop*, but not much. At least she's still there, albeit with a Wallasey name.

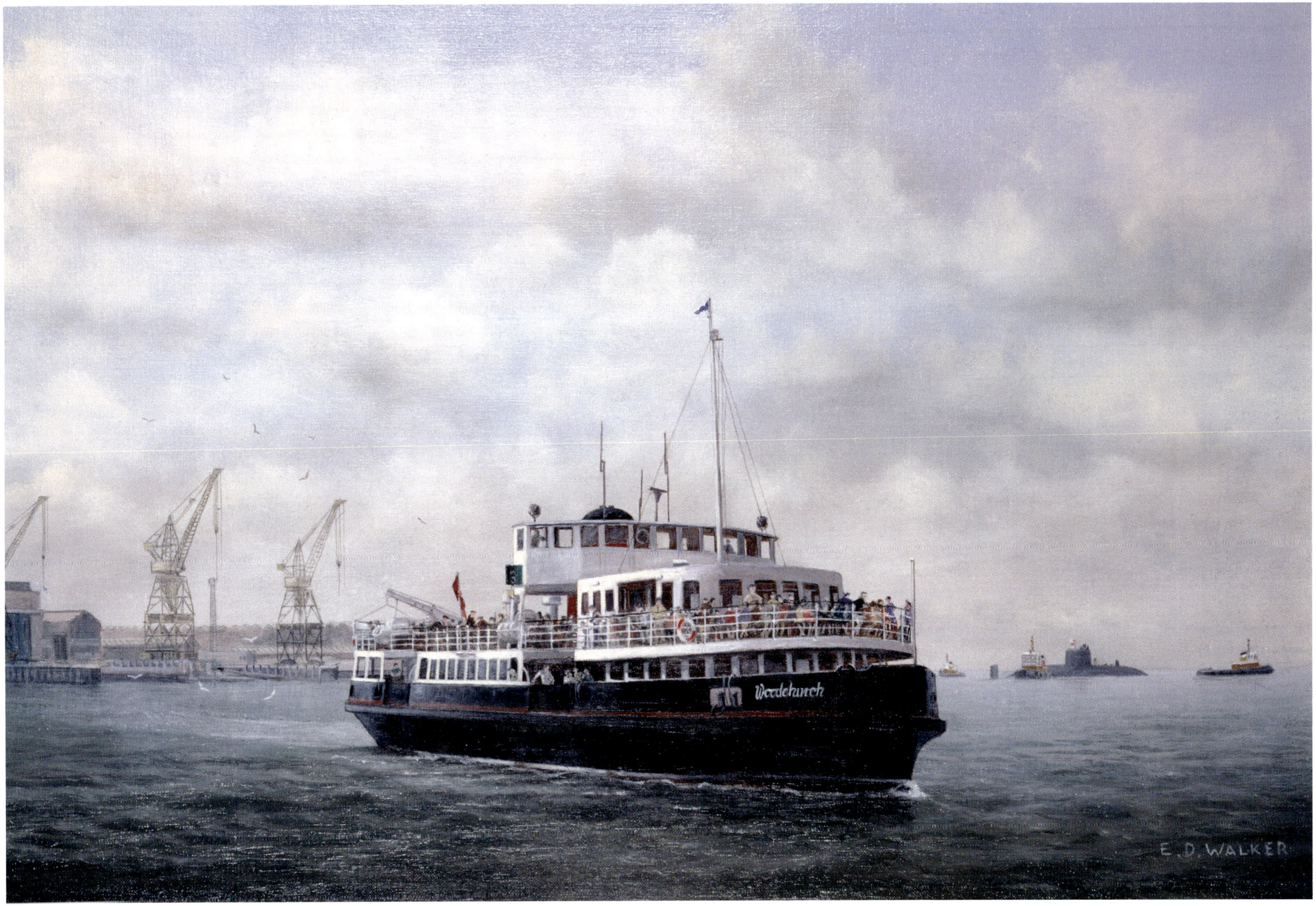
Woodchurch
E. D. WALKER

Manxman

Cunard was not the only company to use the Mersey and to have red and black funnels: the Isle of Man Steam Packet Company's first vessel entered service in 1830.

At the end of the Second World War, the company had lost a number of vessels and of those which survived some were, like *Tynwald* (III) of 1891, no longer at the technological cutting edge. The need to build was urgent, but then so was everyone else's and it took from 1946 to 1955 to get five sister ships, *King Orry* (IV), *Mona's Queen* (IV), *Tynwald* (V), *Snaefell* (V), *Mona's Isle* (V) and *Manxman* (II) into service.

All were built at Cammell Laird's and all measured about 2,500 tons, with a length of 329.7 ft and a beam of 47.2 ft. All carried about 2,300 passengers. All were propelled by steam turbines, but one of the few significant variations was that *Manxman's* turbines were fed superhet steam and had double reduction gearing, resulting in higher efficiency both thermally and mechanically.

The only obviously visible difference within the class is that some had more promenade deck windows than others. These were the last IOMSP vessels built without a drive-on drive off capability for carrying cars or motor bikes, which continued to be swung aboard in cargo nets until the arrival of *Manx Maid* (II) in 1962.

Manxman was, like most Isle of Man boats, a pretty little ship, with the elegance of a great north Atlantic liner miniaturised. But by 1982 good looks were not enough: the ability to carry cars and bikes was pretty essential, and of course landlubberly passengers were beginning to expect ships to be fitted with effete luxuries like stabilisers, of which Manxman was innocent. One may joke, but it is possible to have an extremely rough trip to the Isle of Man.

Strange delusions can afflict apparently rational people when confronted with a pensioned-off ship, especially if it is both pretty and of manageable size. One of the commonest is that it would make a peculiarly attractive floating hotel/conference centre/restaurant/night club and the annals of failed ventures in ship preservation are strewn with examples, of which *Manxman* alone has provided three.

Out of service she went into business in Preston, and failure there resulted in her being towed to Liverpool in 1990 where she failed again. Surely Hull, in 1994 would prove third time lucky? Lying there disused she suffered a fire and in 1997 she moved to Sunderland where she has lain, looking very sad indeed, ever since.

Now there is a new, and hopefully more promising, prospect that she might survive, owing to an initiative by the Manxman Steamship Company (established 2003) which is hoping to bring her back to Birkenhead for restoration in the full knowledge that she will not be able to pay her own way in business terms – and with an apparently realistic estimate of the costs involved. They are starting from the right place!

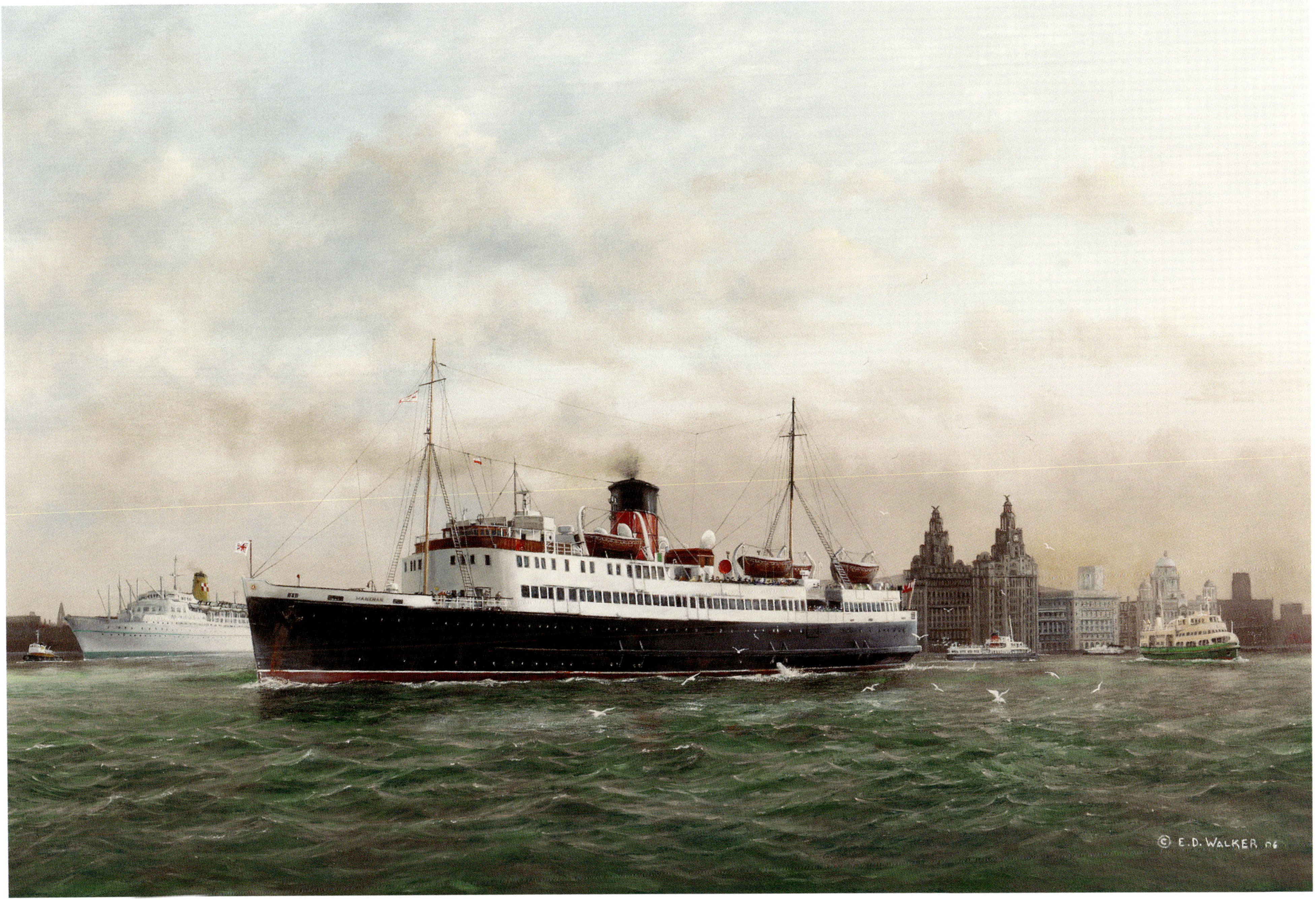
© E.D. WALKER

Planet Lightship

The first vessel of which there is definite record as to ownership by the Trustees of the Liverpool Docks was the 'floating light' *Good Intent* which, under powers granted in the Dock Act of 1811, was placed on what was later known as the 'North West Station', in 1813. Growing trade, changes in the fairly complex channels and increasing concern about accidents to shipping led to extra light vessels being placed until, between 1874-1912, there were five on station with a total complement of 57 men. Thereafter, improvements, especially to the embanking of the channels, made navigation easier and enabled the abolition of the North West Station and the gradual replacement of all the other vessels except for one at the Bar with large floating (unmanned) beacons.

But there were spare boats too: this was because in fog or storm light vessels were quite frequently run down by moving vessels and either sunk or sufficiently damaged to require serious repairs back in port. This happened on average very nearly once a year, whence the need for spares. One particular vessel, the *Comet*, was sunk three times. Being a member of a light vessel's crew was no soft option: they had, by definition, to remain accurately on station, so could not take evasive action when at risk of being run down, and, if one or more anchors yielded through storm or collision, they had no engines with which to manoeuvre back into position. There must have been times when their skippers wished for a torpedo tube or two to deploy in their own defence.

Planet was built by Philip & Son of Dartmouth in 1961. She is quite a substantial little ship, 133 ft long by 26ft breadth. Around that time there was a glut of rivetting-grade steel, which is why *Planet* shares that archaic form of assembly with the Runcorn road bridge. She had a crew of seven, on a 'two weeks on, two weeks off' basis. Conditions were by now much better than those described above, and *Planet* never got run down. The fact that she did not have any propulsion did not mean she had no engine room: on the contrary she had two diesel engines to provide power for the 685,000 cp light, two more to provide compressed air for her various hoists, winches and capstan and two more to work the fire/emergency pumps.

1972 was the year of a painful capital re-organisation of the port resulting from the collapse of the Mersey Docks & Harbour Board and the formation of the Mersey Docks & Harbour Company. In the cost-cutting which followed, the elimination of 14 jobs by the deployment of an overgrown kitchen timer to switch a light on and off was obviously going to appeal. *Planet*, already the last manned lightvessel in the country, was supplanted by a 55ft diameter 'Large Automatic Navigational Buoy'. She moved to a couple of other stations away from the Mersey before ending her active (albeit now unmanned) service with ten years in the Channel Isles in 1989.

The breaker's yard beckoned, but the Mersey Light-vessel Preservation Society are hopeful that they can carry out *Planet's* restoration at an estimated cost of £375,000. They intend to get her back to her original appearance by removing the heli-deck which was added in her Guernsey days (proper Liverpool seafarers could supply her or change crews by boat without getting seasick!) and to use her partly as an exhibit in her own right and partly as a home for the exhibition of historic marine radio and related equipment.

The vessels in the background are the Cunard liner *Sylvania*, the last of four sisters brought into service on the 'slow routes' between 1954 and 1957, and an Isle of Man ferry.

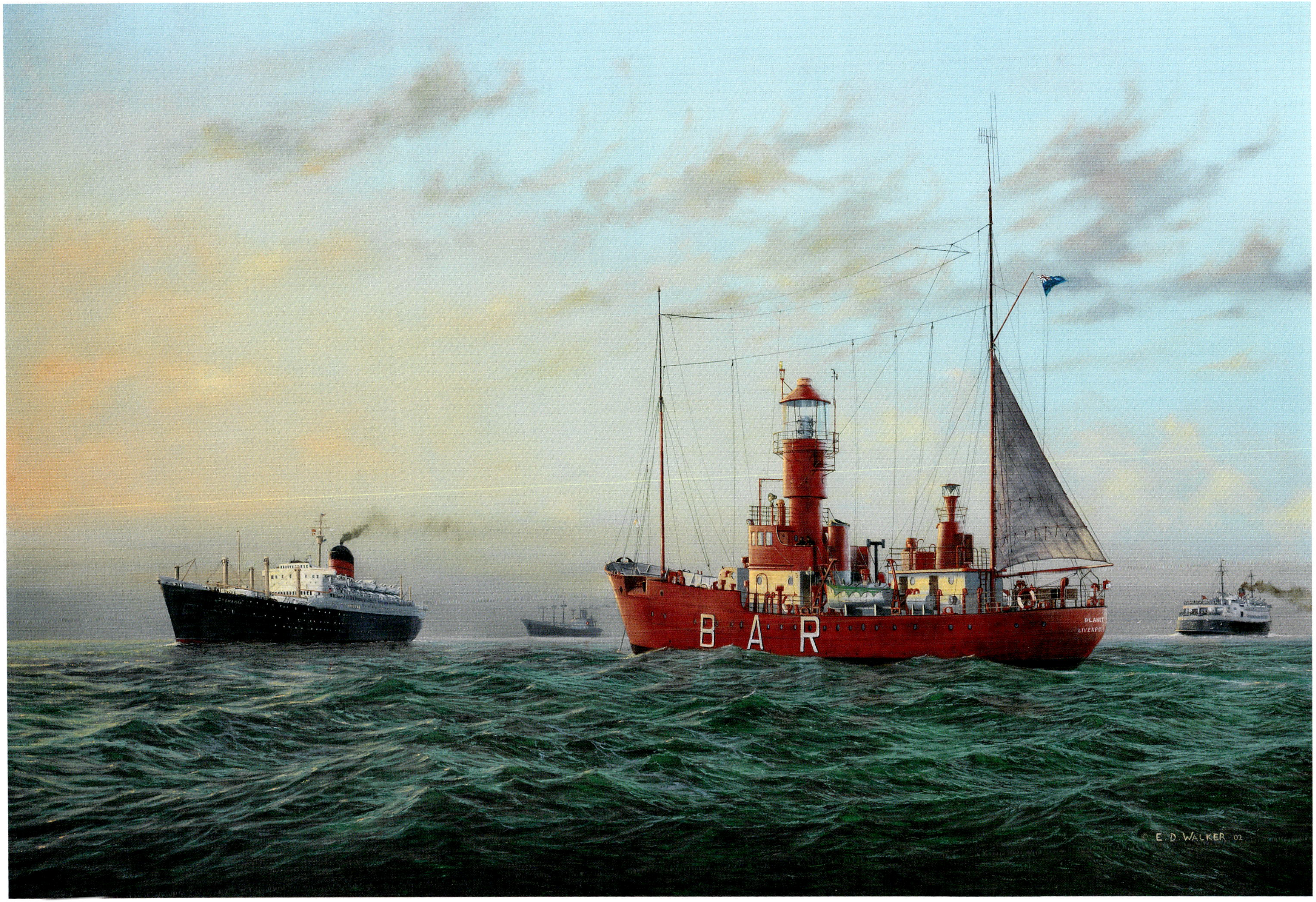
B A R
© E.D. WALKER 02